The
A to Z of Georgian London

Introductory Notes by
Ralph Hyde

HARRY MARGARY, LONDON
in association with Guildhall Library, London
1981

ISBN 0 903541 34 3

www.harrymargary.com

Printed in Great Britain by Headley Brothers Ltd The Invicta Press Ashford Kent and London

CONTENTS

A
PROPOSAL,

By *John Rocque*, Surveyor, and *John Pine*, Engraver,

For Engraving and Printing, by SUBSCRIPTION,

A New, Accurate, and Comprehensive PLAN of the

CITIES of London and Westminster,

AND

BOROUGH of Southwark,

WITH

The contiguous Buildings, from an actual Survey thereof: Which Survey was begun in *March* 1737, is now carrying on, and will be compleated about *September* next. Immediately after which, the Engraving will be put in Hand, and finished with all possible Expedition.

This Plan will be contained in 24 Sheets of the best Imperial Paper, being near 13 Feet in Length, and 6 Feet and an Half in Depth, and will extend from West to East, on the North Side, from beyond *Mary-bone* Turnpike, by *Tottenham-Court*, the *New-River-Head*, *Hoxton* and Part of *Hackney* to near *Bow*: From thence, Southerly, by the Eastermost Parts of *Mile-End* and *Lime-House*, cross the River *Thames* to *Deptford* Road; from whence the Southern Side will extend Westerly, by *Newington* and *Vaux-Hall*, to that Part of *Surrey* which is opposite to *Chelsea-College*; which Building, together with some Part of *Knights-Bridge* and *Hyde-Park*, will be included in the Western Limit, which closes with the Northern beyond *Mary-bone*.

The Space comprized within this Compass, will contain above ten thousand Acres of Ground: And, as it will be laid down by a Scale of 200 Feet to an Inch, the Plan will admit not only of an exact Description of all the Squares, Streets, Courts, and Alleys, in their true Proportions, but likewise of the Ground Plots of the several Churches, Halls, publick Buildings, and considerable Houses and Gardens; and will likewise comprehend a Survey of so much of the Country, with the several Roads and Foot-paths crossing it, and remarkable Objects contained in it, as lies within the above-mentioned Bounds: Which, it is presum'd, will fill up the vacant Space more usefully, as well as more agreeably, than by crouding the Plan with unmeaning Ornaments.

The Method follow'd in making this Survey has been, by ascertaining the Position and Bearings of the Churches and other remarkable Buildings, by Trigonometrical and other Observations from the Tops of Steeples, Towers, and other Places, whence such Buildings are visible; by taking the Angles at the Corners of Streets, &c. with proper Instruments, and measuring the Distances by the Chain: And by comparing, from Time to Time, the Position of Places, found by this last Method, with the general Observations before-mentioned, so as to correct the one by the other.

The Price will be Three Guineas: One to be paid down at the Time of Subscribing, and Two more on the Delivery of the Work.

Note, Tho' the Plan is of so large a Size, by rolling it up on a Roller, to the Cornish of the Wainscot, it will not interfere with any other Furniture; and yet, by the Means of a Pully, it may be let down for Examination at Pleasure.

And a small Plan will be given to such who bind up the Sheets in a Volume, for the Sake of presenting a View of the Whole at once.

Subscriptions are taken in by JOHN PINE, Engraver, in *Old Bond-street* near *Piccadilly*; and by JOHN ROCQUE, Surveyor, at the *Canister* and *Sugar Loaf* against *Queen's-Head-Court* in *Great Windmill-street* near the *Hay-Market*.

THE MAKING OF JOHN ROCQUE'S MAP

John Rocque's survey of mid-eighteenth century London, which we have adapted for this publication, may be said to have originated in Leicester Square. It was here that on 3 March, 1737/8 George Vertue, engraver of a copy the Elizabethan 'Agas' map and Leake's post-Fire City survey, revealed his 'grand design for an Ichnographical Survey or Map of London and all the suburbs' to two fellow antiquaries, William Oldys and Joseph Ames.[1] No thorough-going survey of London had been carried out since the publication of William Morgan's 'London Survey'd' fifty-six years earlier. New editions of Morgan's map had been issued in c. 1692, 1698, c. 1720, and 1732. Several derivatives and a plethora of reduced plagiarisms of it had been published. But London in the early Georgian era, thanks to the expanding population and the enterprise of West End landowners, was spreading rapidly. Now there was an urgent need for a completely fresh survey. Vertue already had a surveyor in mind for this great undertaking—John Rocque—'but Mr. Rocque and he are not yet come to an agreement', recorded William Oldys in his diary.

Rocque's origins are obscure. He was born of Huguenot parents who had fled from France and had settled in Geneva.[2] At some point before 1734 he arrived in England. His brother, Bartholomew, established himself at Waltham Green as a gardener. John at first described himself as a *dessinateur de jardins* and surveyed the gardens of royalty and the aristocracy chiefly in the vicinity of London. His first known survey was of Richmond House, Gardens, Park and Hermitage carried out in 1734 for Frederick, Prince of Wales. Between that date and 1738 he completed surveys of Wanstead Park, Chiswick House and Gardens, Kensington with the Palace and Gardens, South Dalton, Weybridge, Wrest, Esher, Claremont Park, Hampton Court, and Windsor. All these plans were executed in the florid rococo style favoured by Frederick. Small versions of them appeared in a volume of *Vitruvius Britannicus*, dedicated to the Prince of Wales, which Rocque and Badeslade published in 1739. None of these garden plans really posed the problems, nor anything like the challenge, that would be involved in surveying what was, after all, the largest city in the world.

The surveying begins

By the autumn of 1739 Rocque had commenced work on the survey of the metropolis. George Vertue, curiously, was no longer in the picture, the task of engraving the map having been assigned to George II's chief engraver of seals, John Pine. This transfer of responsibility, if such it was, may well have been for the good. Pine was a friend of William Hogarth and a portrait of him may be found in Hogarth's 'Gates of Calais' where he features as the fat friar. His engraving output included a ceremonial of the installation of the Knights of Bath (1725), and ten large plates of the House of Lords tapestries (1739) which recorded the engagements and destruction of the Spanish armada. He ran a print shop in Old Bond Street which later moved to Piccadilly opposite Burlington House, and later still to King Street, Soho. In 1743, before work on the London map had been completed, he would be appointed Bluemantle pursuivant-at-arms in the Heralds' College where he seems to have taken up residence. Thus, in addition to engraving the map and providing the bold decoration so beloved by the contemporary map-purchasing public, Pine, with his reputation in high places, was in a position to attract many influential patrons and subscribers.

On 16 October, 1739 Pine and Rocque very sensibly sought the support and patronage of the Corporation of London.[3] Pine attended the meeting of the Court of Aldermen in person. In order to demonstrate the intended size and style of the map he exhibited a rough drawing of it. This obviously impressed the aldermen who immediately resolved to give the cartographic venture full support. Deputy aldermen, the common councilmen, and citizens of London generally were called upon to co-operate fully with Rocque and Pine. Ward beadles were commanded to assist the mapmakers by locating for them the precise course of their ward boundaries. Permission was granted for the two men to publish the aldermanic order. This they did in the columns of the *London Daily Post and General Advertiser* on the following day.

Civic support effectively secured, Rocque and Pine set to work on the survey in earnest. With the aid of a theodolite supplied by the noted Strand instrument-maker, Jonathan Sisson,[4] bearings were taken from a number of steeples and other prominent landmarks. Angles were also taken at the corners of streets and the streets measured with a chain. On at least one occasion the surveyors were accompanied by two prominent fellows of the Royal Society, Martin Folkes and Peter Davall, later President and Secretary of the Society respectively. In a glowing testimonial they assured the public:

> Having seen what is already done of the new Survey of London undertaken by Mr. Rocque and Mr. Pine, having been inform'd of their manner of proceeding, and having been present at the taking some remarkable Measures, and at the Verifying of several of the principal Angles; we are enabled to declare, That we are satisfied with the same, and that we think we may justly recommend it as a Work of great Use, likely to to be performed with Judgement and Exactness, and well deserving Encouragement.[5]

Problems encountered

In *c.* 1740 Proposals were issued confidently predicting that the survey begun in March 1737/8 would be completed in September next.[6] Immediately after this the engraving would be put in hand and finished with 'all possible Expedition'. The price of the 24-sheet map would be three guineas, one guinea to be paid at the time of subscribing and the other two on delivery. The truth of the matter was, though, that Rocque and Pine were in difficulties. Their principal problem was probably that of lack of experience in undertaking a survey of these proportions. Distances taken when measuring the streets, they later admitted, were at this stage refusing to tally with distances calculated trigonometrically. There was nothing for it but to draft their map all over again and this they did, Folkes and Davall reassuring the public with a second testimonial.[7] Place-names too were producing many headaches. No fewer than 5,000 had to be established, verified, and meticulously plotted onto the draft of the map. The only certain rule with place-names, they found, was 'to reduce the whole to the Standard of custom' and the practice they adopted therefore was to record names on the spot as the survey progressed and then to compare them with the form they had taken in previous documents (unspecified). When discrepancies showed up 'enquiry was made into the Cause of it and the truth cleared up with as much exactness as possible' the authors claimed.[8]

Five more years were to elapse before the great London map was ready for publication. In the meantime Rocque moved from his address at the 'Canister & Sugar Loaf' in Great Windmill Street, Soho, to premises 'next ye Duke of Grafton's Head in Hyde Park Road'—to the Hyde Park Corner of Piccadilly in other words.[9] He embarked on a number of other surveys. He had surveyed the village of Wrington in the Mendip Hills, Somerset in 1738.[10] Now he surveyed the nearby city of Bristol. This map, like the London one, was splendidly engraved by John Pine who modelled it on Rousel's map of Paris, 1730.[11] Bristol Corporation rewarded Benjamin Hickey, the local bookseller who published the four-sheet map in 1743, with a grant of twenty guineas.[12] Rocque also surveyed Exeter. To ensure that their citizens co-operated to the full the Exeter Corporation followed the example of the City of London and furnished Rocque with an 'Advertisement'.[13] They balked at giving financial assistance however. The Exeter plan, published in 1744, was engraved by R. White who also engraved a survey undertaken by Rocque at about the same time of the house and gardens of the Earl of Pembroke at Wilton. Yet another provincial town surveyed by Rocque whilst the London map was in progress was Shrewsbury. This plan, engraved by Richard Parr and dedicated to Viscount Pulteney of Wrington, was published in 1746.

But Rocque's largest and most time-consuming project was a second London wall-map which he had commenced in 1741. This was to take in the country ten miles around London and to be drawn on a scale of 1,000 feet to the inch or approximately five-and-a-quarter inches to the mile. Eight feet long and six feet broad it was to consist of sixteen sheets. The first sheet of it appeared in January 1744. Potential subscribers were encouraged to repair to Hyde Park Road where they could inspect the original drawing of the complete map hanging in Rocque's shop.[14] Sheets appeared at about six-weekly intervals until July 1745 when Rocque announced that he was 'indispensably oblig'd to go into the country for a few months', one assumes to carry out the Shrewsbury survey.[15] The remaining four sheets were to be engraved in his absence and he would correct and finish them on his return. Sceptics were advised to visit Richard Parr, the engraver, in Howard Street behind the Strand, and see for themselves how the work was progressing. Rocque kept his promise. The remaining sheets were published early in 1746.

Completion and publication

Every effort was now being made to complete the 24-sheet plan of London proper. On 2 May, 1746 new Proposals were printed and advertised in the *General Advertiser*. The surprise in the Proposals was the publishers' names. No longer were they given as John Rocque and John Pine. Rocque's name had been dropped to be replaced with that of John Tinney. It is possible that Rocque, in publishing Exeter, Shrewsbury, and London and 10 Miles Round, had over-stretched his financial resources. John Tinney, a successful printmaker in Fleet Street, may have been called in to inject capital into the venture and save it from collapse. Proofs of the sheets, joined to form wall-maps, were hung up in Pine and Tinney's print shops, and the publishers added the following plea in their advertisement:

> As so large a Work, tho' performed with the greatest Care, may still possibly not be wholly free from some Inaccuracies and Omissions, the Proprietors will think themselves oblig'd to the Curious, who shall point out

such to them, and they promise that on such Information, the particular Parts in Question shall be examined on the Spot, and the proper Alterations made, that nothing shall be wanting to make the work Correct as possible. And the Publication of the Work depending on its receiving the necessary Corrections, the sooner any Gentlemen is pleas'd to give such Information, the greater will the Obligation be esteemed and acknowledged.

As a final check 'proper persons' were sent out to every corner of London carrying sheets of the map and making sure that the topography depicted on those sheets corresponded with reality.[16]

The intention was to dedicate the map to the Fleet Street banker, Alderman Sir Richard Hoare, whose term of office as Lord Mayor was due to expire in November 1746, and to his fellow aldermen. There was a necessity somehow then to have it published during Hoare's mayoralty. Imprint details were engraved on the copper plates in October (the actual day of the month was not supplied), and on the 21st, eighteen days before the swearing in of Sir Richard's successor, Pine and Tinney attended the Court of Aldermen where they presented the City fathers with what must have been a set of proofs. The aldermen ordered the map to be hung in the Guildhall Justice Rooms, and instructed the Chamberlain of London to present the map-makers with a gift of £50.[17]

Strictly speaking the map was not published until 1747. In April of that year Pine and Tinney expressed their thanks to the gentlemen who had inspected the map and pointed out errors.[18] Incorporating such corrections had further delayed publication but the map really was now finished and printing off. It would be ready in May. On 27 June, 1747 the map was at last announced in the *General Advertiser* as being available to subscribers. Copies for non-subscribers became available in November by which time an index volume had also been published.[19] Inevitably there was some confusion in the public mind between the two Rocque maps of London. An advertisement in 1749 implored customers to note the difference between the two 'that they may not have the latter imposed on them for the former as has often been the case'.[20]

The map

John Rocque's 'Plan of the Cities of London and Westminster and Borough of Southwark' measured six-and-a-half feet by thirteen, encompassed an area of 10,000 acres, and was drawn to a scale of 200 feet to the inch or twenty-six inches to the mile. Its borders and cartouche design owed much to Louis Bretez's 20-sheet map of Paris which had appeared eight years earlier. The decoration was bold, splendidly confident yet not overpowering. Compared with Nolli's multi-sheet map of Rome published in 1748 it appears positively restrained. Unlike Bretez's Paris, which is a bird's-eye view, Rocque's London is an ichnographical plan. Obviously the map is far more detailed than any other London map of the period yet the user should be warned that it is not one hundred per cent comprehensive. Certain alleys, yards, and closes, the existence of which can be established from printed or manuscript sources, may not be represented on it. Not all place-names are supplied either. 'Hyde Park Road' where Rocque had his premises is not named for example. Public buildings, palaces, and a few great houses are shown on the plan. No attempt is made, though, to show all the individual buildings as Ogilby and Morgan had succeeded in doing on their map of the City in 1676. That the scale of the map was large enough to accommodate that information was demonstrated by Richard Horwood in his map of London of 1792–99, and John Rocque himself on his Dublin plan of 1753. Interestingly, Westminster Bridge is depicted as if complete and open for traffic. The name of Charles Labelye, its Swiss designer, is to be found in the subscription list in the index volume.

The plan is made up of twenty-four imperial sheets. A contemporary catalogue advises would-be purchasers to join them together as one map, to back the whole with canvas, to attach it to a roller and pulley, and to fix it to the cornice of the wainscot 'in such a manner that it may not interfere with other furniture, and it may be let down for examination at Pleasure'.[21] It might also, the catalogue suggests, be made into a beautiful and useful screen. Few today have room in their homes to accommodate a map of such proportions, fitted up on a roller, adapted to form a screen, or even bound up into a volume. Our hope is that in its new *A to Z* format Rocque's survey of the London of George II, William Hogarth, Dr. Johnson, and Lord Lovat may prove to be a convenient and handy reference tool for scholars and amateur historians alike.

REFERENCES

1. *A Literary Antiquary: Memoir of William Oldys Esq., Norroy-King-at-Arms, together with his Diary* . . . (London: Spottiswood & Co. 1862), p. 19
2. 'John Rocque, Engraver, Surveyor, Cartographer, and Mapmaker', by J. Varley, *Imago Mundi*, V (1948), pp. 83–91
3. C[orporation of] L[ondon] R[ecord] O[ffice], Rep. 143, pp. 162–3
4. See Folkes and Davall's second testimonial, dated 24 July, 1742, transcribed in Rocque's *Alphabetical Index*, 1747
5. Transcribed on p. 2 of Rocque and Pine's Proposals, *c.* 1740 (copy in Chetham Library, Manchester)
6. ibid., p. 1
7. *Alphabetical Index*, p. vi
8. ibid., p. vii
9. Established by Hugh Phillips in 'John Rocque's Career', *London Topographical Record*, XX (1952), pp. 12–13

10. Survey in Bristol R.O. See 'A Map of Wrington in 1738', by H. P. Chambers, C. Truman, and E. M. West, in *Wrington Village Records* (University of Bristol Dept. of Extra Mural Studies, n.d.)
11. See Hickey's advertisement in *Oracle*, 30 April, 1743. His Proposals appeared in the same newspaper on 18 Dec., 1742
12. Bristol R.O., Audit Bks., 1743/4, p. 57
13. Devon R.O., Act Bks., vol. 14, 1731–66, fo. 11b, 112a
14. *Daily Advertiser*, 15 Jan., 1744
15. ibid., 16 July, 1744
16. *Alphabetical Index*, p. vii
17. C.L.R.O., Rep. 150
18. *General Advertiser*, 25 April, 1747; *London Evening Post*, 30 April–2 May, 1747
19. *General Advertiser*, 13 Nov., 1747
20. ibid., 22 Feb., 1749
21. *Sayer and Bennett's Catalogue of Prints for 1775* (London: Holland Press, 1970)

ACKNOWLEDGEMENTS AND PUBLISHER'S NOTE

The author of the above notes wishes to express his gratitude to Mr. Donald Hodson who so generously passed on to him numerous advertisements for Rocque's London maps discovered by him in eighteenth-century newspapers.

The publisher would like to express his appreciation to Mr. A. D. Baxter for permitting his particularly fine copy of Rocque's 'Plan of the Cities of London and Westminster and the Borough of Southwark' to be reproduced for this *A to Z*. He is also extremely grateful to Mr. John Fisher, Assistant Keeper of Prints & Maps at Guildhall Library, for the invaluable assistance he gave with the editing of the Index, and to Mr. Alan Hodgkiss for drafting the Key Map.

In order to create this *A to Z* Rocque's twenty-four sheets have each been photographically reduced by 1:0.56, the original references have been removed from the decorative borders, and the resulting spaces in the borders have been filled with matching fleurons. A grid has been superimposed over the map areas and new references added in the margins. The base-map represents No. 96 (2) in James Howgego's *Printed Maps of London*.

FURTHER READING

Georgian London
BESANT, Sir Walter, *London in the Eighteenth Century* (London: Adam & Charles Black, 1902)
GEORGE, Mary Dorothy, *London Life in the XVIIIth Century* (London: Kegan Paul, 1925)
PHILLIPS, Hugh, *Mid-Georgian London* (London: Collins, 1964)
PHILLIPS, Hugh, *The Thames about 1750* (London: Collins, 1951)
RUDÉ, George, *Hanoverian London, 1714–1808* (London: Secker & Warburg [1971])
SUMMERSON, Sir John, *Georgian London* (London: Barrie & Jenkins [1970])

John Rocque's Maps
ANDREWS, J. H., 'The French School of Dublin Land Surveyors', *Irish Geography*, vol. V (1967), pp. 275–92
ANDREWS, J. H., *Two Maps of 18th Century Dublin and its Surroundings* (Lympne: Harry Margary, 1977)
COBB, Hugh, 'Four Manuscript Maps Recently Acquired by the British Museum', *Journal of the Society of Archivists,* vol. IV (1973), pp. 646–52
GLANVILLE, Philippa, *London in Maps* (London: Connoisseur [1972])
HOWGEGO, James, *Printed Maps of London, c. 1553–1850* (Folkestone: Dawson [1978])
PHILLIPS, Hugh, 'John Rocque's Career', *London Topographical Record*, vol. XX (1958), pp. 9–25
ROCQUE, John, *A Topographical Survey of the County of Berkshire*. Facsimile published by Harry Margary, with notes by Paul Laxton, 1973
ROCQUE, John, *An Exact Survey of the City's of London Westminster, ye Borough of Southwark and the Country near 10 Miles Round London*. Facsimile published by Harry Margary, with notes by J. L. Howgego, 1971
ROCQUE, John, *A Plan of the Cities of London and Westminster and Borough of Southwark*. Facsimile published by Harry Margary, with notes by J. L. Howgego, 1971
SNOWDEN, W. Crawford, *London 200 Years Ago* (London: Daily Mail, 1948)
VARLEY, John, 'John Rocque, Engraver, Surveyor, Cartographer, and Mapmaker', *Imago Mundi*, vol. V (1948), pp. 83–91

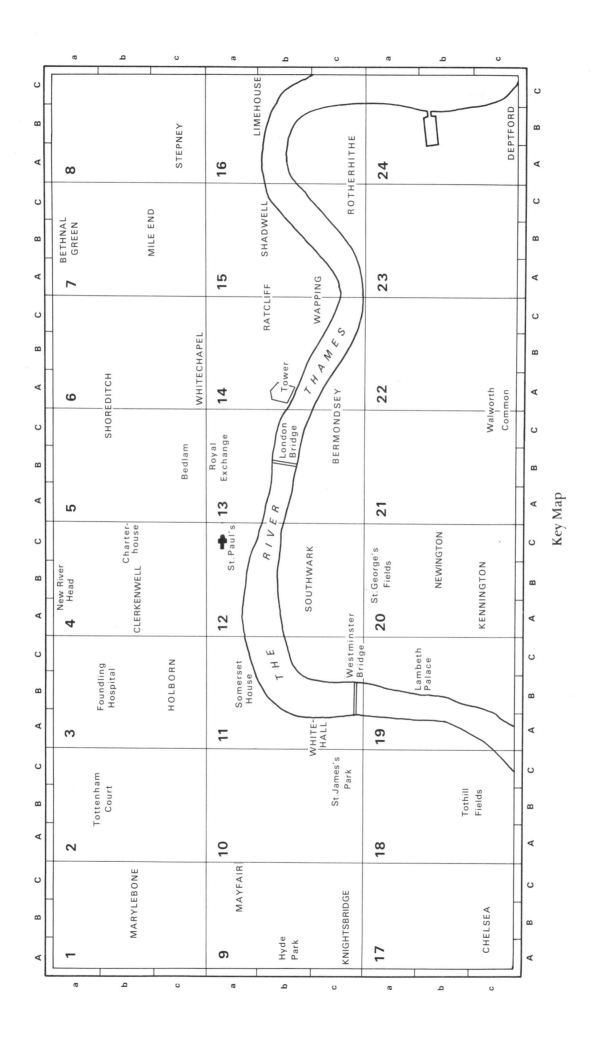

Key Map

1

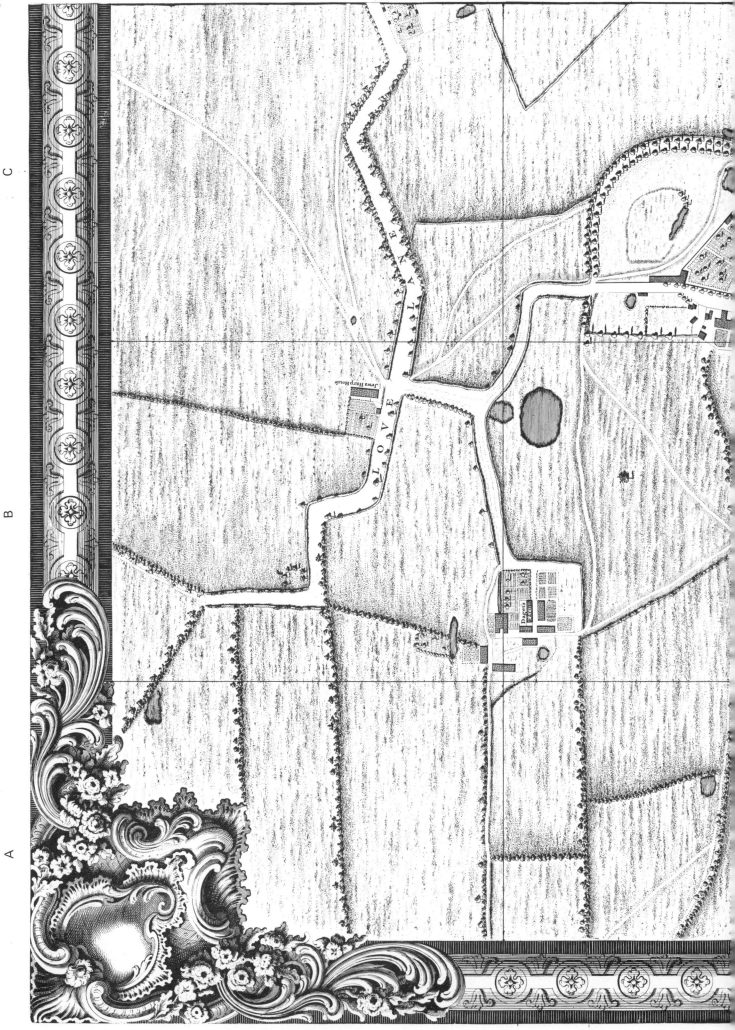

LOVE LANE

Jews Harp House

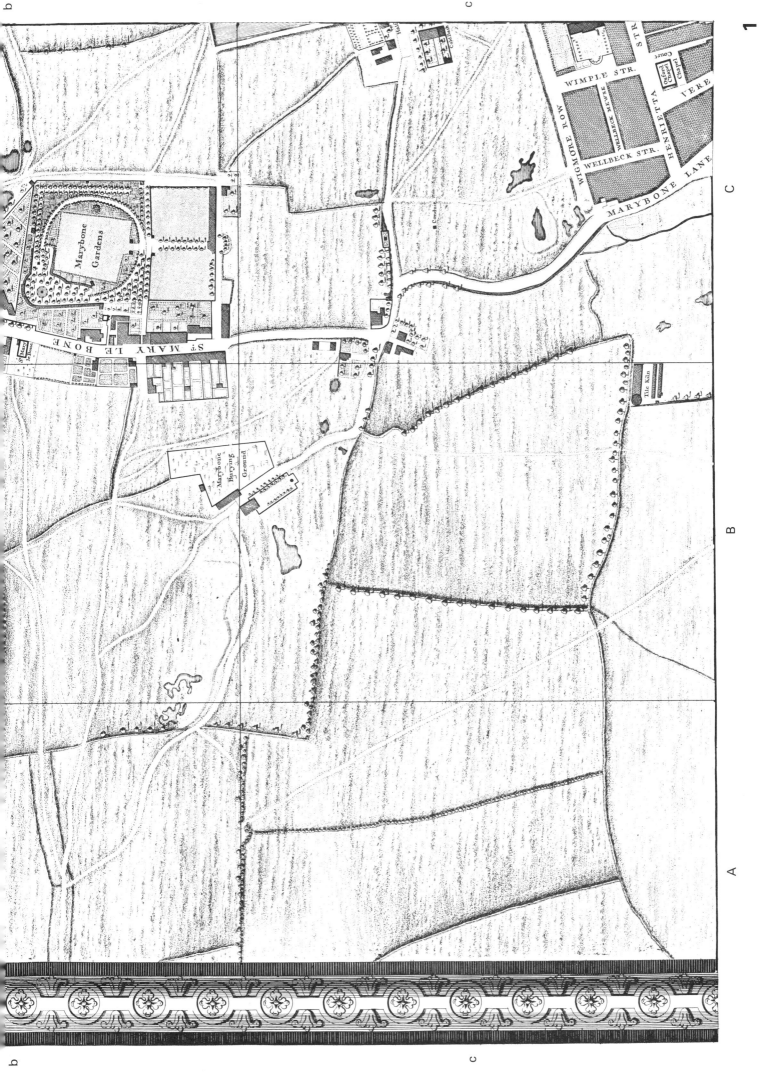

1

2

A

B

C

a

b

ROAD TO HIGHGATE

TOTTENHAM COURT

Turnpike

Pound

GREEN LANE

Bittons Farm

Farthing Py House

Queens Head

T

a

b

4

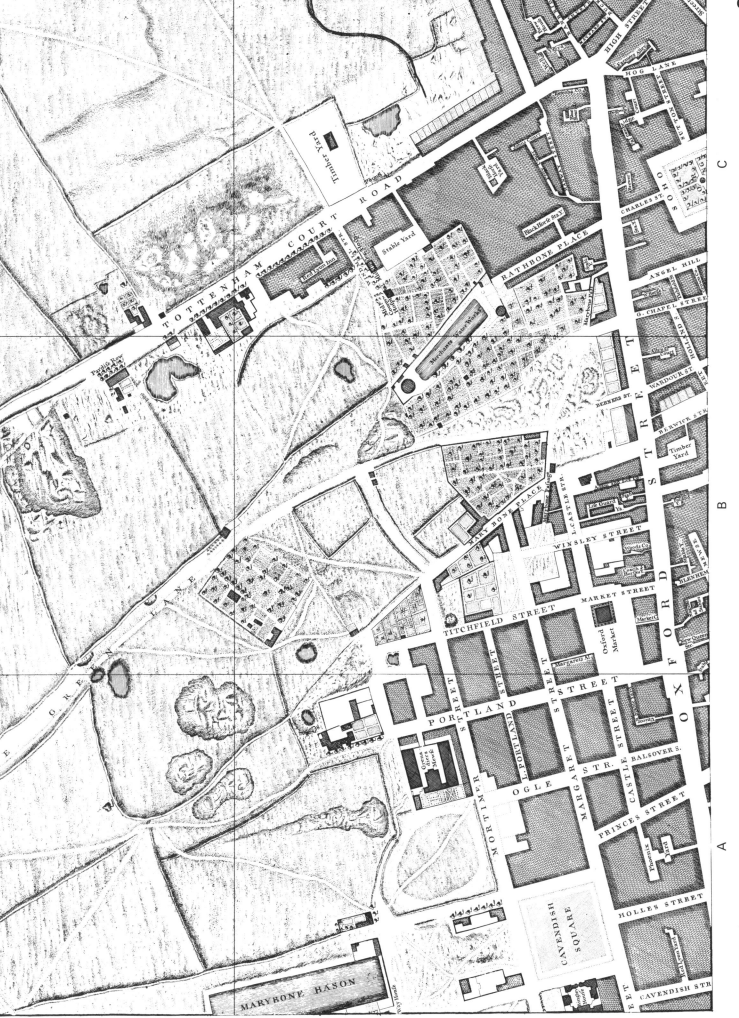

2

C

B

A

HIGH STREET

STREET

HOG LANE

CHARLES ST.

SOHO

ANGEL HILL

G. CHAPEL STREET

WARDOUR ST.

BERWICK STR.

HOLLAND S

Timber
Yard

BERNERS ST.

RATHBONE PLACE

Black Horse Sta Y

Stable Yard

Red Lyon Inn

TOTTENHAM COURT ROAD

Merchants Lane Works

MARY BONE PLACE

L. CASTLE STR.

WINSLEY STREET

Life Guard
Ya

Coach
Horse Y

Woods Co

MARKET STREET

Oxford
Market

Market

TITCHFIELD STREET

Margaretz Alc

BLENHEI

New Quebec
Str.

Timber Yard

Pound

PORTLAND STREET

L. PORTLAND STREET

OGLE STREET

MARGARET STREET

CASTLE STREET

BALSOVERS S.

PRINCES STREET

Phoenix Yard

GREEN LANE

Grena
diers
Mewse

MARYBONE BASON

Way House

CAVENDISH SQUARE

HOLLES STREET

CAVENDISH STR.

Paradise Row

OXFORD

MORTIMER STREET

PORTLAND

Timber Yard

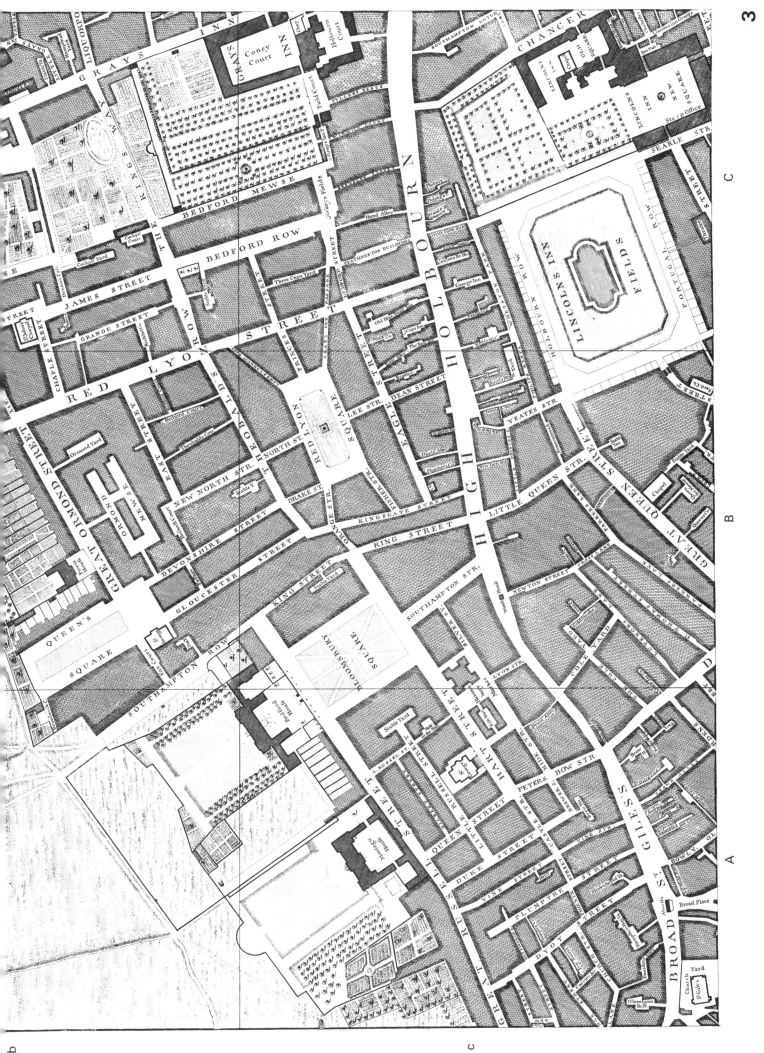

GRAYS INN

LIQUORPO

G

Coney
Court

GRAYS INN

Chap.

Holbourn
Court

Field Court

CHANCER

SOUTHAMPTON BUILD

LINCOLNS INN

Chapel

OLD

NEW SQUARE

SQUARE

LINCOLNS INN

Stamp Office

KET

Devils Inn Grpes

BEDFORD MEWSE

Jockey's Fields

Hand Alley

LINCOLNS INN FIELDS

SEARLE STR

PORTUGAL ROW

SEARLE STREET

C

BEDFORD ROW

FEATHERSTON BUILDING

HOLBOURN

Three Cups Yard

BEDFORD ROW

JAMES STREET

Cockpit Yard

Dennis Fats

Cockpit Court

THE KING'S WAY

CHAPLE STREET

GRANGE STREET

St Helens Chapel

RED LYON STREET

THEOBALDS STREET

PRINCES STREET

BEDFORD STREET

GRAYS INN PASSAGE

GRAYS INN LANE

LEATHER STREET

Old Blue Inn

3 Cups Inn

The N

EAGLE DEAN STREET

LEE STR.

George Inn

Unicorn Br Ho.

H

YEATES STR.

Davis Alley

New Inn Str

LINCOLNS INN FIELDS

HOLBOURN ROW

JAMES STREET

LYON STREET

Ormond Yard

GREAT ORMOND STREET

Bedford Court

EAST STREET

THEOBALDS STREET

Theobalds Cou.

NEW NORTH STR.

Stable Y.

DEVONSHIRE STREET

DRAKE ST.

ORANGE STR.

RED LYON SQUARE

FISHER STR.

Plumbers Co.

KINGSGATE STREET

H

LITTLE QUEEN STR.

GREAT QUEEN STREET

FARKERS LANE

Chapel

Queen

ORMOND MEWSE

Powis Ho.

Powis House

QUEEN'S SQUARE

GLOUCESTER STREET

KING STREET

Stable Yard

KING STREET

KING STREET

HIGH

Watch House

SOUTHAMPTON STR.

SILVER ST

NEWTON STREET

KINGS WAY

GOLD

COLE YARD

STREET

QUEEN'S SQUARE

Fox Court

SOUTHAMPTON ROW

BLOOMSBURY SQUARE

LYON STR.

Brew

D

Bedford House

Montague House

HART STREET

GILES

STREET

RUSSELL STREET

L. RUSSELL ST.

LITTLE RUSSELL STREET

Sheep

BOW STR.

PETERS.

BREWERS STR.

DRURY LANE

Almo Ho.

BROAD ST.

Broad Place

QUEEN STREET

CASTLE STREET

VINE STR.

A

DUKE STREET

VINE STREET

PLUMPTRE STREET

DYOT STREET

White Lyon Br.H.

Church Yard

St Giles

4

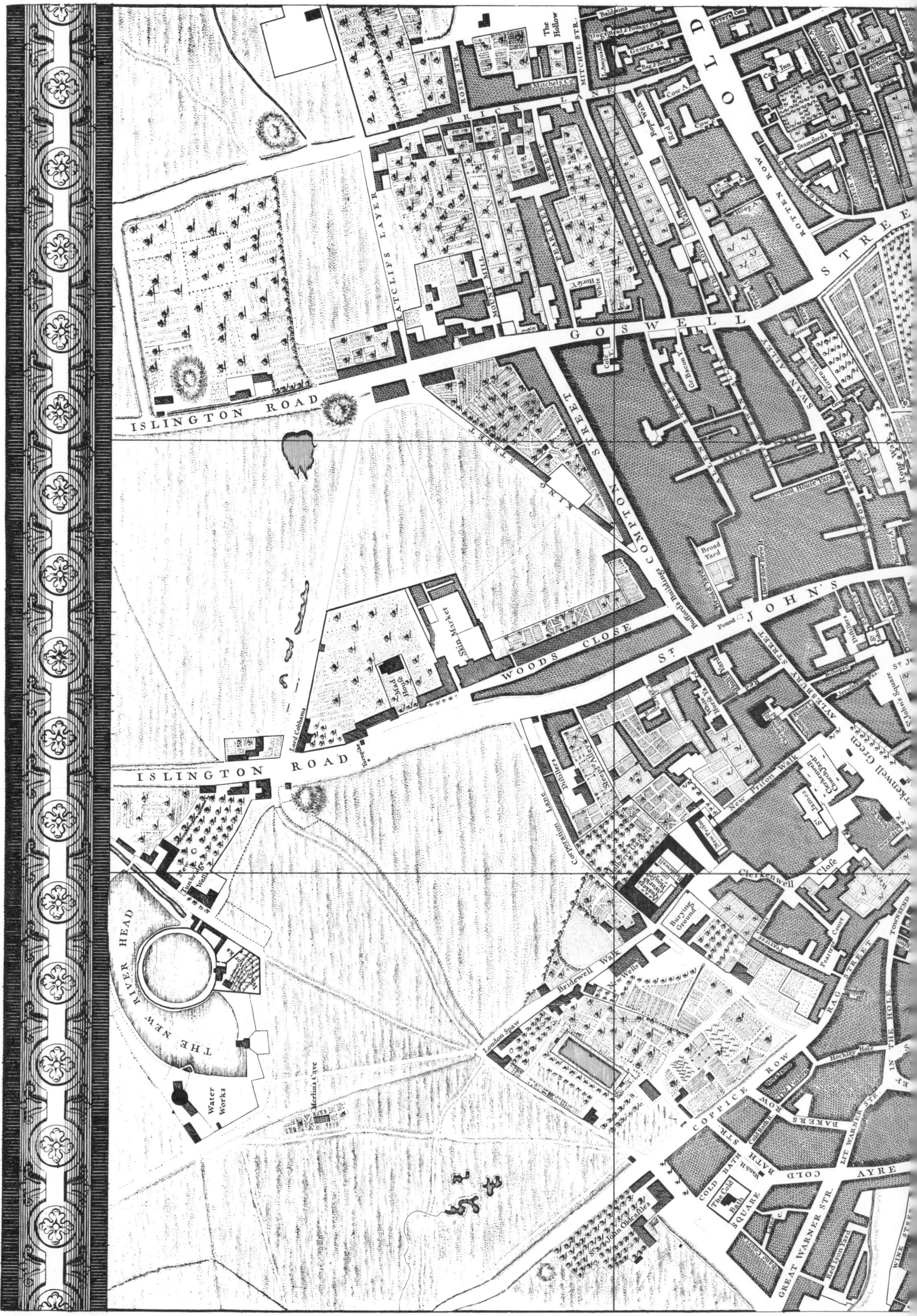

a   b

C

B

A

ISLINGTON ROAD

ISLINGTON ROAD

GOSWELL STREET

RATCLIFS LAYER

BRICK LANE

ROSE ST

MITCHEL STR

MOUNT MILL

The Hollow

COMPTON STREET

KING STREET

WOODS CLOSE

Skin-Market

ST JOHN'S STREET

Broad Yard

Pound

AYLESBURY STREET

NEW PRISON WALK

Clerkenwell Green

Clerkenwell Close

THE NEW RIVER HEAD

Water Works

Merlins Cave

Tunbridge Wells

London Spaw

Bridewell Walk

New Wells

Burying Ground

COPPICE ROW

BAKERS ROW

RAG STREET

COLD BATH

COLD BATH SQUARE

GREAT WARNER STREET

LIT WARNER STR

WINE STREET

AYRE

SWAN ALLEY

COTTEN ROW

a   b

8

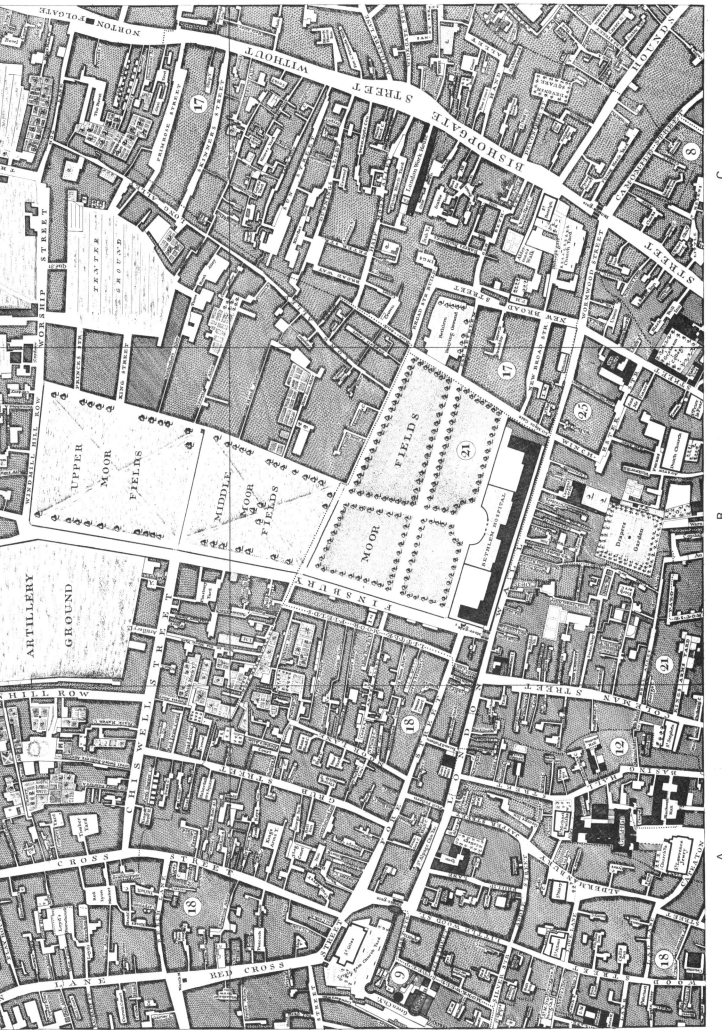

A   B   C

a   b

COATES LANE

Court Farm

St Matthew
Church
Yard

WOOD STREET

SILVER STREET

FULLER STREET

Oakey C

HARE STREET

HARE MARSH

THE HILL

EDWARDS s.

ST JOHNS STREET

FLEET STREET

SATCHELLS RENTS

JAMES STR.

Thomas Str.

Black Bird Alley

NEW G

CHURCH STREET

BRICK   L

VIRGINIA ROW

TYSSEN STR.

ROSE SPR. STREET

Bacon Str.

BACON STREET

SWAN STREET

SCLATER STREET

PHENIX STREET

CRABTREE LANE

NEW COCK LANE

FINK STREET

FARTHING

TURVILE STREET

CLUB ROW

CRABTREE LANE

NICHOL STREET

NEW NICHOL STREET

OLD NICHOL STREET

ANCHOR STREET

SILK STREET

COCK LANE

COCK LANE

AUSTINS STREET

THE ROAD TO HACKNEY

Farmer's Yard

Shoreditch
Burying Ground

Distillers

St Leonard
Shoreditch Church Yard

Almshouse School

Watch H

Brew Ho.

S H O R E D I T C H

a   b

12

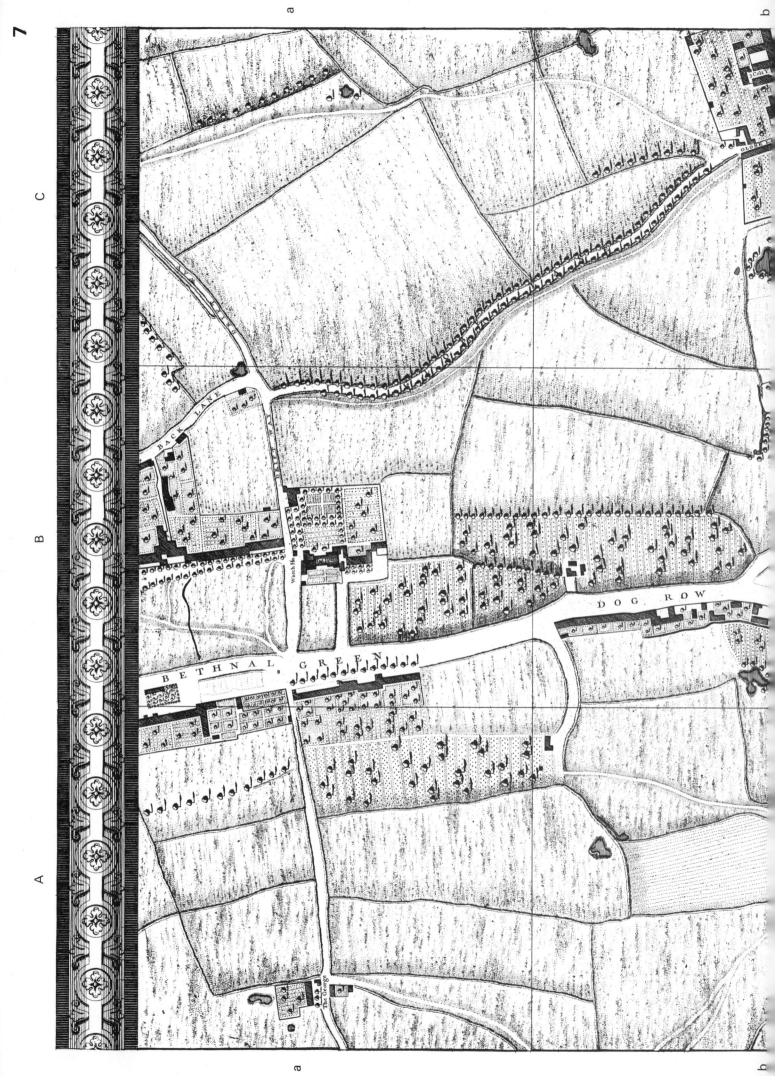

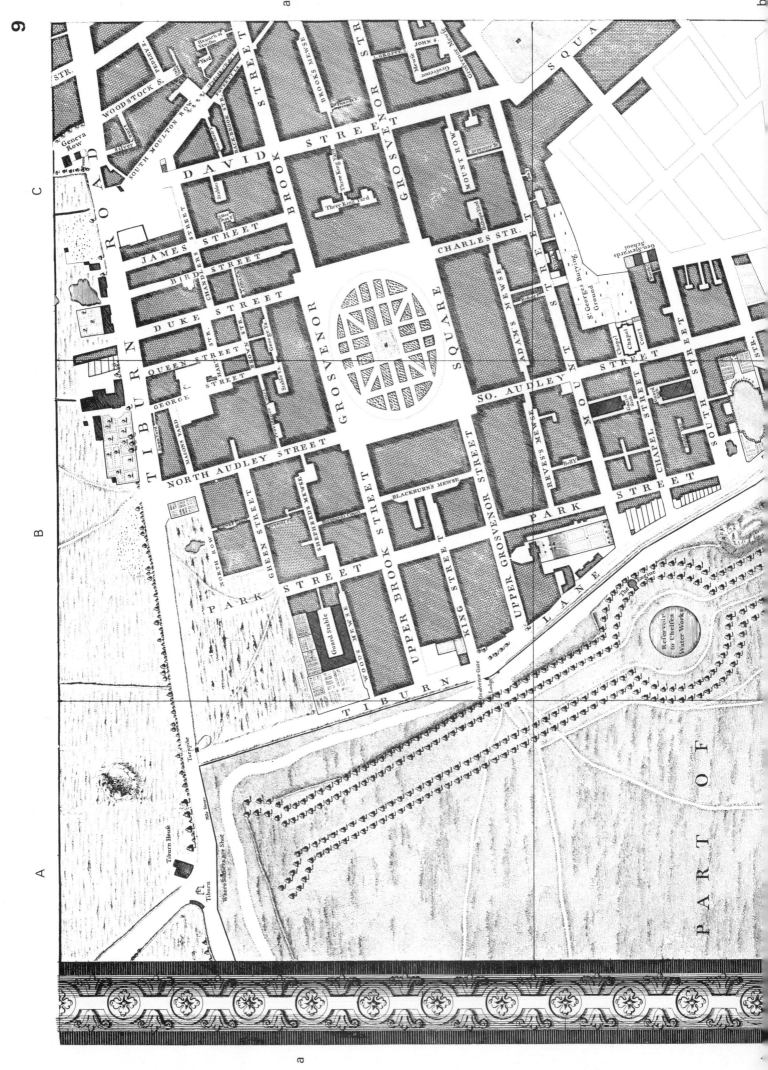

9

a

b

C

B

A

SQUA

SQUARE

ROAD

TIBURN

DAVID STREET

BROOK STREET

GROSVENOR STR

BROOKS MEWSE

WOODSTOCK S.

Geneva Row

SOUTH MOULTON ROW

JAMES STREET

BIRDERS STREET

DUKE STREET

QUEEN STREET

GEORGE

MASONS YARD

Haunch of Venison Yard

Stable

Three King Yard

Three King Yard

CHANDERS STREET

BROWN STR.

Stable Yd

GROSVENOR SQUARE

NORTH AUDLEY STREET

PARK STREET

GREEN STREET

UPPER BROOK STREET

KING STREET

UPPER GROSVENOR STREET

SHEPHERDS MEWSE

WOODS MEWSE

Guard Stable

BLACKBURN'S MEWSE

NORTH ROW

CHARLES STR.

MOUNT ROW

SO. AUDLEY STREET

ADAM'S MEWSE

MOUNT STREET

REVES'S MEWSE

PARK STREET

CHAPEL STREET

SOUTH STREET

St. George's Burying Ground

Gen. Stewards School

Chapel

JOHN S.

PART OF

TIBURN

Grosvenor Gate

TIBURN LANE

The Engine

Reservoir to Chelsea Water Works

Tiburn House

Turnpike

Tiburn

18

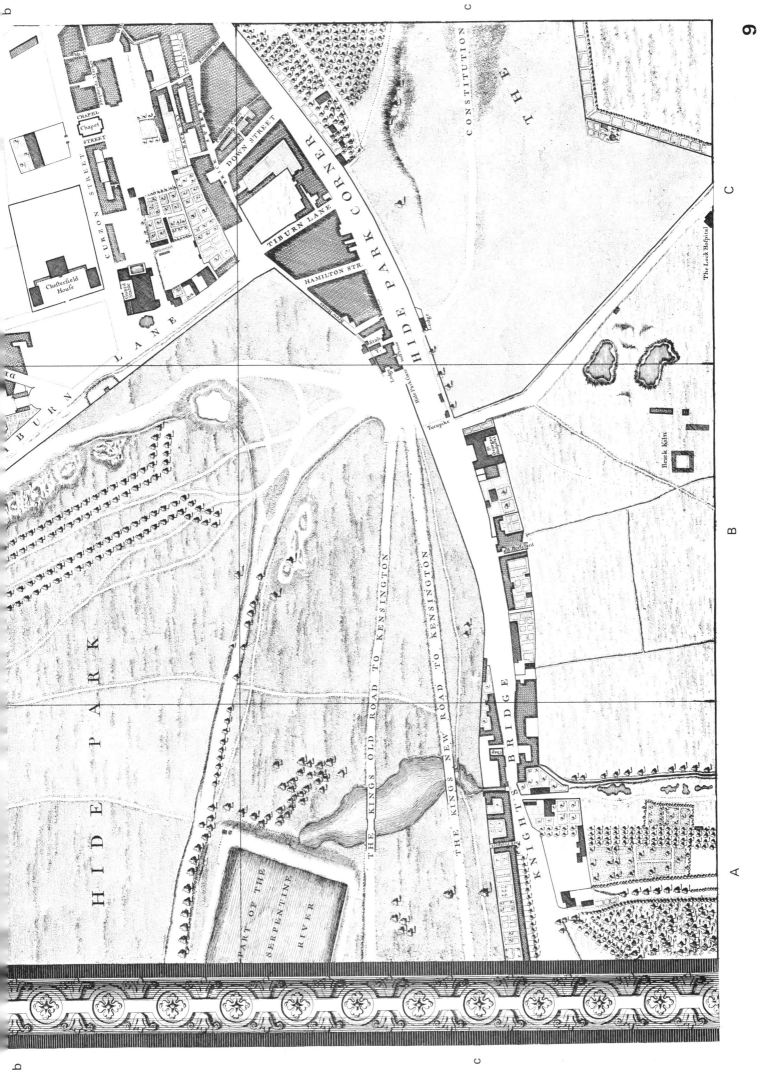

CHAPEL STREET

CHAPEL

Chesterfield House

CURZON STREET

DOWN STREET

TIBURN LANE

HAMILTON STR.

Guard Stable

TIBURN LANE

HIDE PARK CORNER

Hide Park Gate

Lodge

Lodge

Stable

Turnpike

THE

CONSTITUTION

The Lock Hospital

Brick Kiln

St. Georges Hospital

The Horse Yard

HIDE PARK

KNIGHT'S BRIDGE

THE KINGS OLD ROAD TO KENSINGTON

THE KINGS NEW ROAD TO KENSINGTON

PART OF THE SERPENTINE RIVER

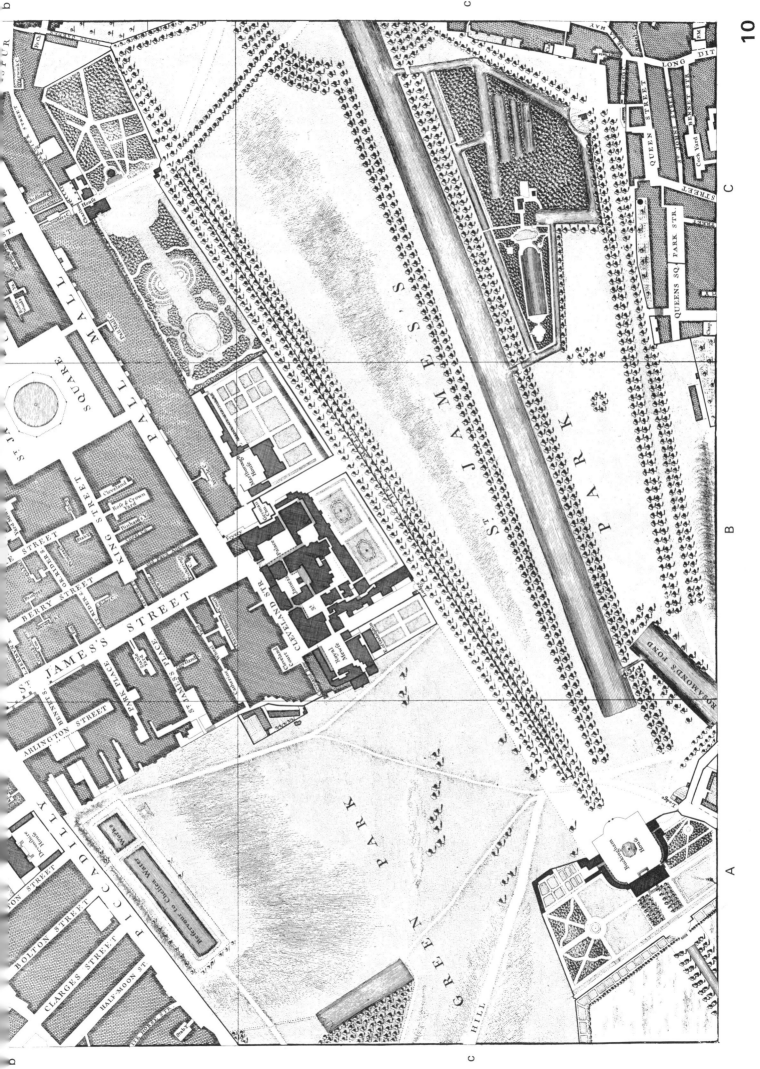

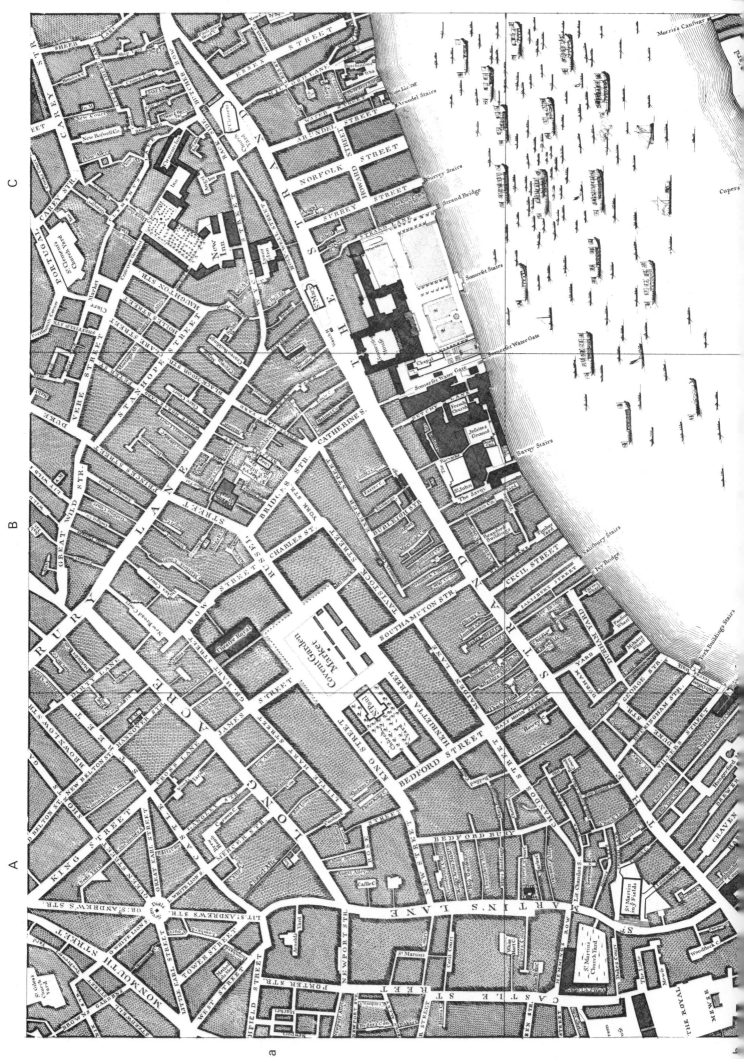

A B C (map grid references)

THE NEW ROAD

LAMBETH

VINE STREET

Timber Yard

Timber Wharf

Little River Side

Crown Court

Stone Wharf

Timber Yard

COLLEGE STREET

Cuper's Gardens

Boreside Green

CABBAGE

NARROW

Kings Arms Stairs

Timber Yard

Timber Yard

Whitening Wharf

Timber Yard

Timber Yard

Timber Yard

Timber Yard

WESTMINSTER BRIDGE

BRIDGE STR.

Westminster Bridge Stairs

White Hall Stairs

Privy Garden Stairs

Manchester Stairs

Hungerford Stairs

Timber Yard

Sand Wharf

Darby Court

CHANNEL ROW

SCOTLAND YARD

MIDDLE SCOTLAND YARD

INNER SCOTLAND YARD

WHITE HALL

Privy Garden

Privy Garden

Chapel

Banqueting Ho.

Cock Pit

WHITE HALL

Admiralty Office

CHARING CROSS

SPRING GARDEN

NEW STREET

Horse Guard

Tilt Yard

Treasury

DOWNING STREET

PARLIAMENT STREET

KING STREET

CHARLES STREET

BRIDGE STREET

NEW PALACE YARD

UNION STR.

ST MAR

SANCTUARY

PARADE

DUKE STREET

Green's Alley

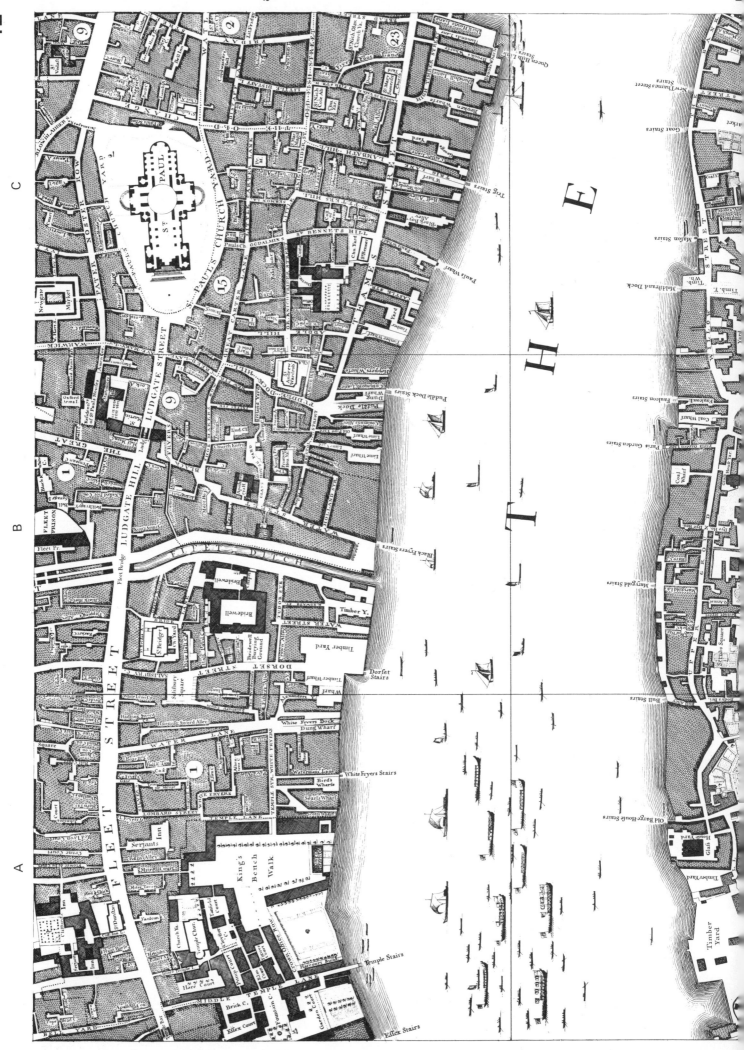

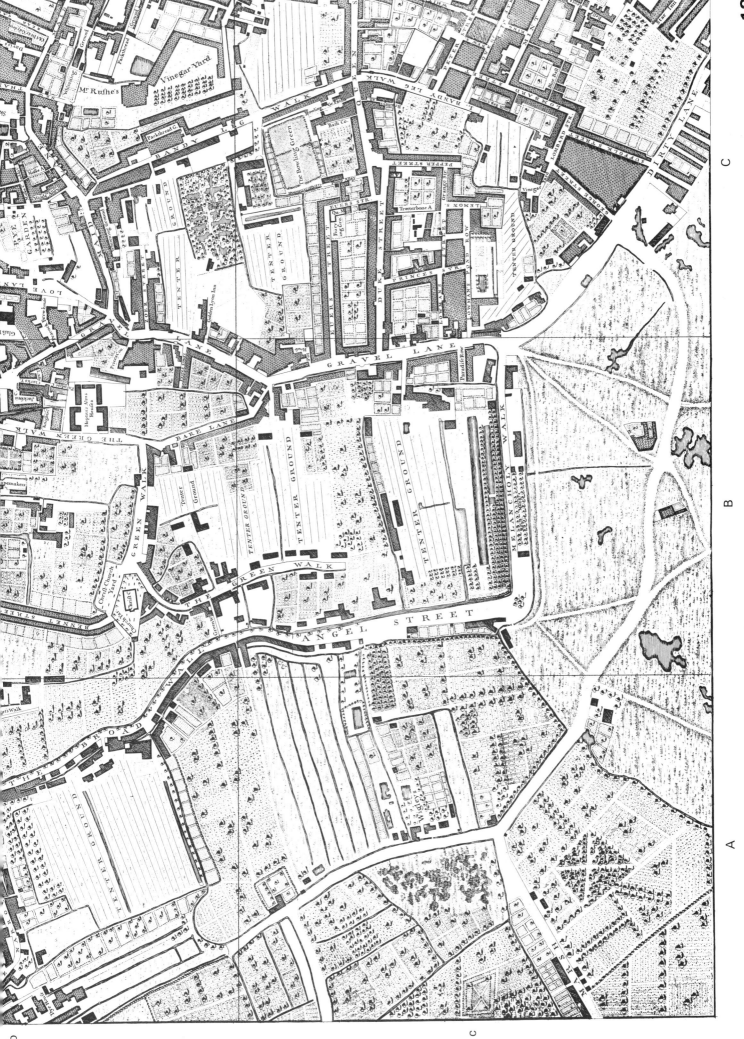

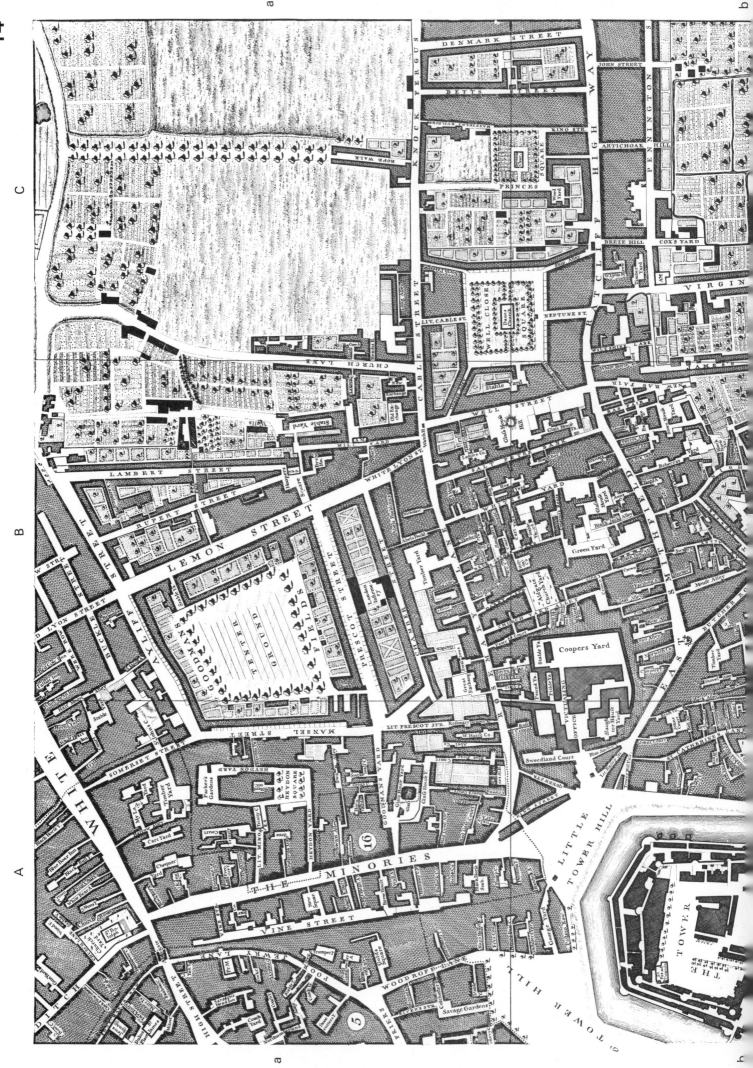

King & Queen Stairs
Timber Wharf
A Dry Dock
Shipwrights

Russels Hill Stairs

Shadwell Dock
Coopers Yard

Pelican Stairs
Boat Builder

King James's Stairs

HANOVER STREET

Hanover Stairs

STAR STREET

Fox and Goo

Coxes Gardens
Mast Yard
Shadwell Dock

New Crane Stairs

Lime Wha

Frying Pan Stairs

King Edwards Stairs

Church Stairs

CHURCH

Burying Ground

St George's
Hospital

PRINCES STREET

SHIP STREET

Timber Yard

WAPPING DOCK

Wapping Dock Stairs

Elephant Stairs

Princes Stairs

PRINCES

NEW MARKET STR

Timber Yard

Coopers Y

Execution Dock Stairs

Wharf

Kings Stairs

BROAD STREET

OLD GRAVEL LANE

Dung

Wapping New Stairs

Redriff Stairs

Queens Head Alley

RED LYON STREET

Anchor and Hope Alley

Well All

Gilham

Well Lane Stairs

a

b

C

B

A

CHURCH YARD

St. Ann

Cowh

SERMON   LANE

SERMON   LANE

ROSE   LANE

ROSE   LANE

WHITE   HORSE   STREET

RATCLIFF SQUARE

LONDON   STREET

THREE COLT STREET

CHURCH

ROPEMAKERS   FIELD

THREE   COLT   STREET

LIME-KILN   DOCK

LIME-KILN   YARD

LIME HOUSE CORNER

THE   ROPE   WALK

QUEEN   STREET

BUTCHER   ROW

Ratcliff Cross

Wharf

Horns Dock

Wharf

Dry Dock

Stone Stairs

Harris's Court

Bear Court

Ship Alley

Nightingal Lane

Spring Stairs

Kidney Stairs

Godwel Stairs

Limehouse Bridge Dock

a

b

b

c

C

B

A

c

14

E HOLE

Shipwrights

White Lead Yard

Limehouse Hole Stairs

Landward Gun Stairs

Timber Yard

Timber Yard

Cuckolds Point

LAVENDER STREET

QUEEN STREET

TRINITY STREET

COVE LANE

Stairs

Shipwrights

LAVENDER STREET

Shipwrights

Shepherd

Shepherd Stairs

JAMAICA STREET

WRIGHT STREET

Stairs at Globe Island

SLUICE STREET

C

B

A

CHELSEA

AVER...

FIVE FIELDS ROW

STRUMBELO

WILDERNESS ROW

Ranelagh Gardens

Chelsea Water Works

THE NEAT HOUSES

College Burying Ground

Morgans Ground

JEWS ROW

BROAD ROW

MAJOR...ROW

GARDNERS ROW

FRANCKLINS ROW

CHELSEA COLLEGE

ROYAL...

A Scale of 1320 Feet, making one quarter of a Mile or two Furlongs.

A Scale of 200 Paris Toises, making 1200 French or 1278¼ English Feet.

Abbreviations.

A. or All. *Alley*.	R. or Re. *Rents*.
Alm.H. or A.H. *Alms-Houses*.	R. or Ro. *Row*.
A.M. *Anabaptist Meeting*.	S. or STR. *Street*.
B. or Build. *Buildings*.	T. *Tavern*.
Bl. *Black. or Blue*.	W. *White*.
K. *Kings*.	Y. or Ya. *Yard*.
L. or LA. *Lane*.	G. or Gr. *Green*.
L. or Lit. *Little*.	R. *Red*.
C.Y. *Church Yard*.	B.G. or Bur. G. *Burying Ground*.
Cou. *Court*.	Sch. *School*.
Chap. *Chapel*.	
Ger.Ch. *German Church*.	
GR. *Great*.	
H. or Hou. *House*.	
H. or Ha. *Hall*.	
I.M. *Independant Meeting*.	
Inn.	
N. *New*.	
O. *Old*.	
P.M. or Pr.M. *Presbyterian Meeting*.	
Q. *Queen*.	
Q. M. *Quakers Meeting*.	

KENNINGTON

Vaux Hall Spring Garden

LAMBETH

White Hart Stairs

Boat Builders

NEW ST.

PLATE GLASS
HOUSE

VAUX HALL

Gun House Stairs

Vaux Hall Stairs

Marble Hall

C

B

A

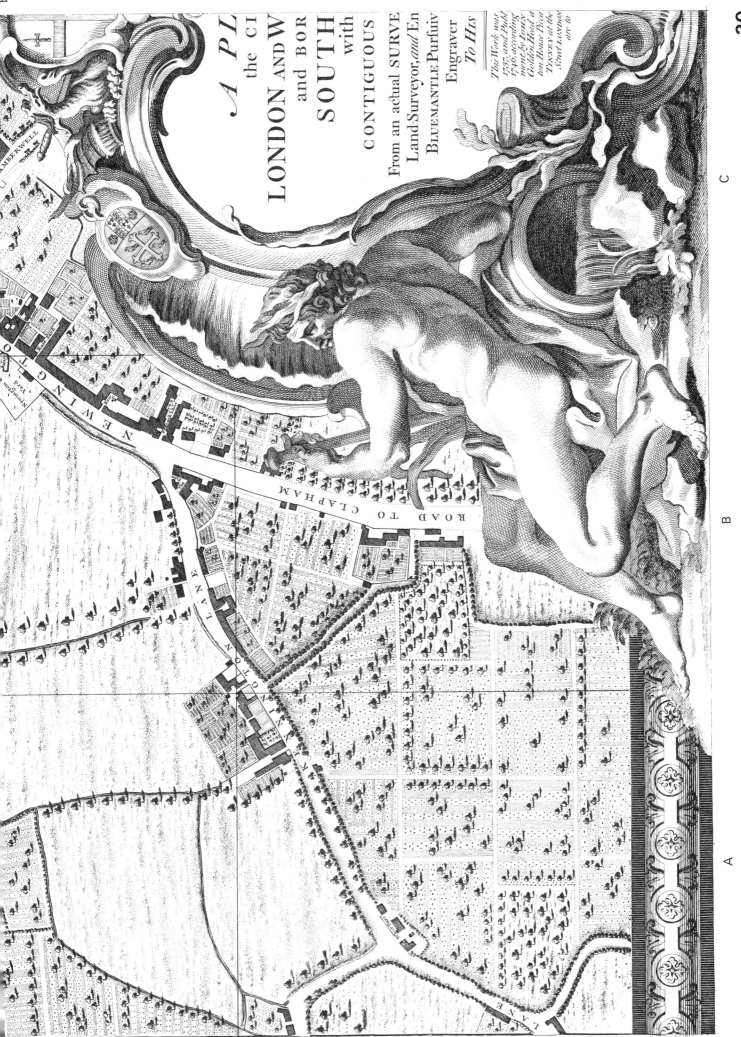

A PL[...]
the CI[...]
LONDON AND W[...]
and BOR[...]
SOUTH[...]
with
CONTIGUOUS

From an actual SURVE[...]
Land-Surveyor, and En[...]
BLUEMANTLE Purfuiv[...]
Engraver
To His

This Work was [...]
1737, and Publ[...]
1746; according [...]
ment by JOHN [...]
Golden Head a [...]
ton House Piaz[...]
VESEY at the [...]
Street LONDON [...]
are to

CAMBERWELL

NEWINGTON

Newington Butts

LANE

ROAD TO CLAPHAM

LANE

A   B   C

CHERRY GARDEN

CROSS STR.

MARYGOLD STREET

C

B

A

a

b

ROPE WALK

ROPE WALK

SALTER

NECKINGER RAOD

ROPE MAKERS WALK

BLUE ANCHOR ROAD

Tanners Yard

The Grange

Tanners Yard

Tanners Yard

Orange Yard

GRANGE WALK

THE GRANGE ROAD

The Ship

FIVE

a

b

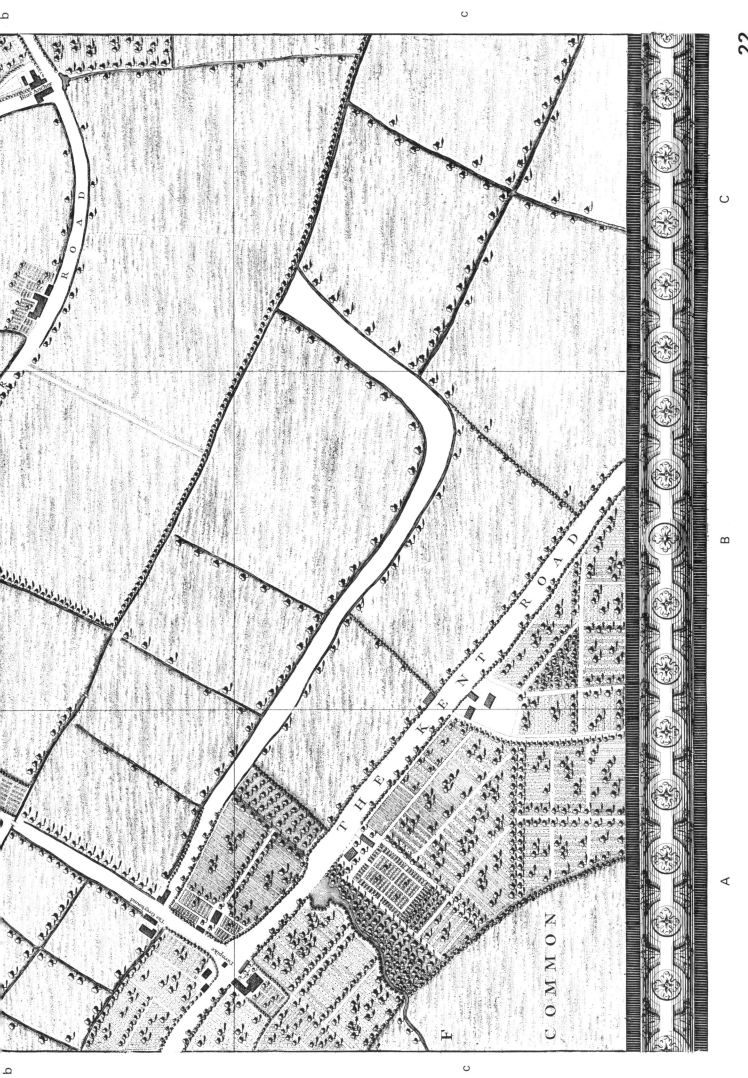

ROAD

The Blue Anchor

THE KENT ROAD

The Gun-ground

The Temple

F

COMMON

C

B

A

c

b

c

b

THE ROAD TO DEPTFORD

To the Rt Honourable

Sr Rich: Hoare Knt:

LORD MAYOR, and Alderman of the Ward of Farringdon without, &

To the Rt worshipful the Court of Aldermen of the City of London, viz:

Aldermen of

WARD		Aldermen of
Bread - street _ 2		Sr Robt: Baylis Knt:
Bridge without		Sr Edwd: Bellamy Knt:
Candlewick _ 3		Sr Jnº Thompson Knt:
Dowgate _ 4		Sr Jnº Barnard Knt:-
Aldgate _ 5		Micajah Perry Esqr:-
Tower _ 6		Sr Danl: Lambert Knt:
Wallbrook _ 7		George Heathcote Esqr:
Lime - street 8		Sr Robt: Willimott Knt:
Farringdn: with 9		Sr Henry Marshall Knt:

RECORDER;

John Stracey Esqr:

Ward.		Aldermen
Bridge within 10		Sr Geo. Champion Knt:
Langborn _ 11		Sr Joseph Hankey Knt:
Bassishaw _ 12		William Baker Esqr:

Sr Jnº Bosworth Knt: Chamberlain. Thos Garrard Esqr: Common Serjant.& Miles Man Esqr: Town Clerk

WARD		Aldermen of
Cheap _ 13		George Arnold Esqr:
Aldersgate _ 14		William Benn Esqr:
Castle Baynard 15		Sr Robt: Ladbroke Knt:
Portsoken _ 16		Sr William Calvert Knt:
Bishopsgate _ 17		Sr Saml: Pennant Knt:
Cripplegate _ 18		John Blachford Esqr:
Cornhill _ 19		Francis Cokayne Esqr:
Billingsgate _ 20		Tho Winterbottom Esqr:
Coleman - street 21		Robert Allsop Esqr:-
Vintry _ 22		Crisp Gascoyne Esqr:
Queenhith _ 23		Edward Davies Esqr:
Cordwainer 24		Edwd Ironside Esqr:
Broad str 25		Tho: Rawlinson Esqr:

This Plan (in Gratitude for ye Assistance received from them in
the Execution of it) is most humbly Inscribed by
their most obedt humbt Servant, John Pine. &
J. Tinney.

N.B. The Figures annexed to the
Names of the Wards in the Dedication,
refer to the Divisions of the Wards in the Plan.

C

B

A

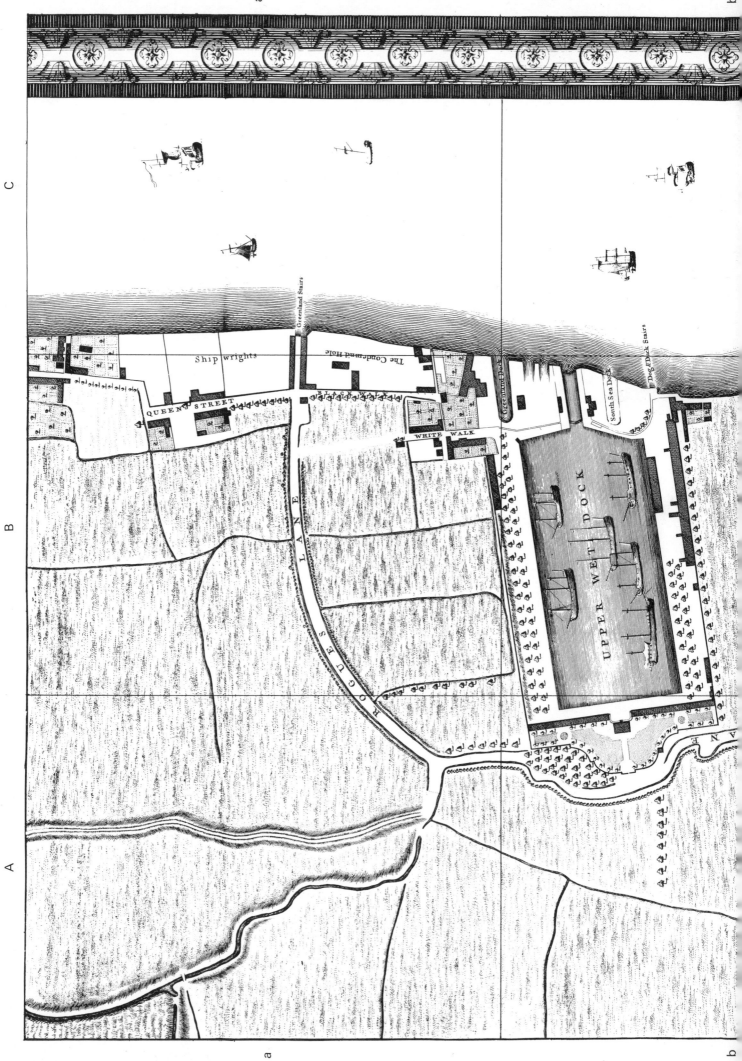

a

b

C

B

A

a

b

Greenland Stairs

Ship wrights

The Conde&nd Hole

QUEEN'S STREET

BLA

WHITE WALK

ROGUES

LANE

Greenland Do

South Sea Dock

Dog & Duck Stairs

UPPER WET DOCK

LANE

b

c

George Stairs

NEW RENTS

Shipwrights

LOWER DOCK

Mill Pond

Angloshire Alley

GROVE STREET

VICTUALING OFFICE WARE HOUSES

RED HOUSE WALL

PART OF THE KING'S YARD

The Plough

ROGUES

LITTLE ROGUES LANE

The Artichoak

B

A

b

c

EXPLANATION OF INDEX

In 1747 Pine and Tinney published their *Alphabetical Index* to Rocque's map as a separate volume. The arrangement of the entries in it was somewhat unhelpful. A list of alleys was followed by a list of courts, which was followed by lanes, streets, miscellanies and so on. To create the index for this *A to Z* Pine and Tinney's entries have been re-arranged to form one alphabetical sequence. The spellings in the original index have been retained except in the following circumstances:

(i) Where inconsistent spelling would result in the separation of place names (e.g. Phoenix, Phenix, Phaenix) places are brought together under the spelling most generally used (Phoenix).

(ii) Where Pine and Tinney used unfamiliar spellings for particularly well-known places (Germain Street, Lyme Street, Hide Park) the present index provides additional entries for the modern spellings (Jermyn Street, Lime Street, Hyde Park). An additional entry is not supplied when the altered spelling would appear next to the original spelling in the alphabetical sequence.

(iii) Where printer's errors would result in entries being misplaced they are corrected (e.g. Green Arbour Court becomes Green Arbour Court).

It needs to be stressed that the index we provide here has not been freshly compiled but basically represents the original mid-eighteenth century index re-arranged more hepfully for the modern user.

PLACE NAME INDEX

Bank End Stairs, Bank Side 13Ab
Bank of England, Threadneedle Street 13Ba
Bank Side, Southwark 12Cb 13Ab
Bank's Yard, Anchor Alley, Bunhill Row 5Ab
Banners Rents, Portpool Lane 4Ab
Bannister's Alley, Broad St. Giles 3Ac
Barbers' Alley, Brown's Lane, Spittlefields 6Bb
Barber's Hall, Monkwell Street 5Ac
Barbican Street, Old Street 4Cb 5Ab
Bare Lane, Gravel Lane 12Bb
Barge Houses, Lambeth 19Ba
Barge Houses, Wapping 14Cc
Barge Yard, Bucklersbury 13Aa
Barking Alley, Seething Lane 13Cb
Barking Alley, Tower Street 13Cb
Barlam's Mewse, New Bond Street 10Aa
Barnaby Street, Tooly Street 13Cc 21Ca
Barnard's Inn, Holborn 4Ac
Barnes Street, Oxford Street 2Cc
Barnett's Yard, Mill Bank 19Aa
Barracks, Savoy 11Ba
Barret's Court, Horsleydown Fair Street 14Ac
Bartholomew Close, Little Britain 4Cc
Bartholomew Court, near Harrow Alley, Houndsditch 6Ac
Bartholomew Court, Throgmorton Street 13Ba
Bartholomew Lane, Threadneedle Street 13Ba
Bartlet's Buildings, Holbourn 4Ac
Bartlet's Court, Bartlet Street 4Bb
Bartlet's Court, Holbourn Hill 4Ac
Bartlet's Passage, Fetter Lane 4Ac
Bartlet's Street, Red Lion Street 4Bb
Barton Street, College Street, Westminster 19Aa
Basing Lane, Bread Street 18Aa
Basinghall Court, Basinghall Street 5Aa
Basinghall Street, Cateaton Street 5Ac
Bath Court, Queen Street 12Cc
Bath Street, Cold Bath Fields 4Ab
Battle Bridge, Mill Lane 13Cb
Battle Bridge Stairs, near Mill Lane 13Cb
Beach Lane, Whitecross Street 5Ab
Beadles Court, Eagle Street 3Bc
Beak Street, Swallow Street 10Ba
Bear Alley, Bride Lane 12Ba
Bear Alley, Fleet Ditch 4Bc
Bear Court, Butcher Row, Radcliff 16Aa

Bear Garden, Bankside 12Cb
Bear Key Stairs 13Cb
Bear and Ragged Staff Inn, Smithfield 4Bc
Bear and Ragged Staff Yard, Whitecross Street 5Ab
Bear Street, Leicester Fields 10Ca 11Aa
Bear Yard, Fore Street, Lambeth 19Bb
Bear Yard, Vere Street, Clare Market 11Ba
Bearbinder Lane, Swithin's Lane 13Ba
Bear's Foot Alley, Bank Side 13Ab
Beauchamp Street, Lether Lane 4Ac
Beaufort Buildings, in the Strand 11Ba 11Bb
Beck's Rents, Ropemakers Fields 16Cb
Beck's Rents, Rosemary Lane 14Bb 14Ba
Bedford Bury, Shandos Street 11Aa 11Ab
Bedford Court, Bedford Street 11Aa
Bedford Court, Red Lion Street, Holbourn 3Bb
Bedford House, Bloomsbury Square 3Ab 3Bb 3Ac 3Bc
Bedford Mewse, by Grays Inn Walks 3Cb 3Cc
Bedford Row, Gray's Inn 3Cc 3Cb
Bedford Street, King Street, Covent Garden 11Aa
Bedford Street, Liquorpond Street 4Ab
Bedford Street, Red Lion Street 3Cc
Bedward's Court, White Street 13Ac
Beech Lane, Whitecross Street 5Ab
Beehive Court, Little St. Thomas Apostles 13Aa
Beer Lane, Thames Street 13Cb
Bell Alley, Austin Frier's 5Bc
Bell Alley, Cannon Street 13Ba
Bell Alley, Coleman Street 5Ac 5Bc
Bell Alley, Dock Head 14Ac
Bell Alley, Golden Lane 5Ab
Bell Alley, Goswell Street 4Cb
Bell Alley, King Street, Westminster 11Ac
Bell Alley, Labour-in-Vain Hill, Thames Street 12Ca
Bell Alley, Lamb Street, Spittlefields 6Ab
Bell Alley, Saffron Hill 4Ab
Bell Alley, Snow Hill 4Bc
Bell Alley, Tooley Street, Southwark 13Bb
Bell Alley, Turnmill Street 4Bb
Bell Alley, Wapping 14Cc
Bell and Bear Alley, Great Eastcheap 13Ba
Bell Court, Gray's Inn Lane 4Ac
Bell Court, St. Martin's le Grand 4Cc
Bell Dock, Wapping 14Cc
Bell Inn, Addle Hill 12Ca

Bell Inn, Aldersgate Street 4Cc
Bell Inn, Coleman Street 5Ac
Bell Inn, Friday Street 12Ca
Bell Inn, Grub Street 5Ac
Bell Inn, Hay Market 10Cb
Bell Inn, Holbourn 4Ac
Bell Inn, Holywell Street 11Ba
Bell Inn, Smithfield 4Cc
Bell Inn, Warwick Lane 4Cc
Bell Inn, Wood Street 5Ac
Bell Lane, White Row, Spittle fields 6Ac
Bell Savage Inn, Ludgate Hill 12Ba
Bell Savage Yard, Ludgate Hill 12Ba
Bell Wharf, Bell Wharf Stairs, Lower Shadwell 15Cb
Bell Wharf Stairs, near Cook Hill, Lower Shadwell 15Cb
Bell Yard, Barnaby Street 21Ca
Bell Yard, Fish Street Hill 13Ba
Bell Yard, Fleet Street 12Aa
Bell Yard, Gracechurch Street 13Ba
Bell Yard, Great Carter Lane 12Ca
Bell Yard, King Street, Westminster 11Ac
Bell Yard, Mincing Lane 13Cc
Bell Yard, Mount Street 9Bb
Bell Yard, St. Margaret's Hill 13Ac
Bell Yard, Stoney Lane 13Ca
Bell Yard, Vine Street 3Ac
Bell Yard, Whitechapel 6Bc
Bell's Alley, St. Catharine's Lane 14Ab
Bell's Rents, Barnaby Street 13Cc
Bell's Rents, Mint Street 12Cc 13Ac
Ben Court, Grub Street 5Ab 5Ac
Bencroft's Hospital, Mile End Old Town 8Ab
Benjamin Street, Red Lion Street 4Bb
Bennet Street, Long Ditch, Westminster 10Cc
Bennet Street, St. James's Street 10Ab 10Bb
Bennet Street, near the Upper Ground 12Bb
Bennet's Court, Drury Lane 11Ba
Bennet's Court in the Strand 11Ba
Bennet's Hill, Thames Street 12Ca
Bennet's Yard, Tufton Street, Westminster 19Aa
Bentinck Street, Berwick Street 10Ba
Berkley Street, Hide Park Road 10Ab
Bernard's Inn, Holbourn 4Ac
Berners Street, Oxford Street 2Cc
Berry Court, Liquor Pond Street 4Ab 3Cb

Berry Court, Love Lane, Wood Street 5Ac
Berry Court, St. Mary Ax 13Ca
Berry Street, near St. James's Street 10Bb
Berry Street, near St. Mary Ax 13Ca
Berwick Street Chapel 10Ca
Berwick Street, Old Soho, Oxford Street 10Ba 18Aa 18Bc
Bethlem Burying Gound, Moorfields Quarters 5Cc
Bethnal Green 7Ba
Bett's Street, Ratcliff Highway 14Ca 14Cb
Bevis Mark, St. Mary Ax 13Ca
Bigg's Alley, Thral Street 6Bc
Bill Alley, Billiter Lane 13Ca
Billingsgate Dock, Thames Street 13Cb
Billingsgate Stairs, Billingsgate, Thames Street 13Bb
Billingsgate, Thames Street 13Cb
Billiter Lane, Leadenhall Street 13Ca
Billiter Square, Billiter Lane 13Ca
Bilson's Farm, near Tottenham Court 2Ab
Bingley House, Cavendish Square 2Ac
Binham's Yard, King Street, St. James's Square 10Bb
Birching Lane, Cornhill 13Ba
Bird in Hand Alley, Cheapside 13Aa
Birdcage Alley, Borough and Mint Street 13Ac
Bird's Court, Philip Lane 5Ac
Bird's Street, Brook Street or Tyburn Road 9Ca
Bird's Street, Green Bank 14Cc
Bird's Wharf, Whitefriers Stairs 12Aa
Bishop of Ely's House 4Ac
Bishop of London's House, Aldersgate Street 4Cc
Bishop's Court, Ailsbury Street 4Bb
Bishop's Court, Chancery Lane 3Cc 4Ac
Bishop's Court, Coleman Street 5Ac
Bishop's Court, Durham Yard 11Bb
Bishop's Court, Fore Street 5Ac
Bishop's Court, Gray's Inn Lane 4Ac
Bishop's Court, Little Old Bailey 4Bc
Bishop's Court, Lothbury 13Ba
Bishop's Court, Old Street 5Ab
Bishops Yard, Charles Street, Grosvenor Square 9Ca
Bishopsgate, Bishopsgate Street 5Cc
Bishopsgate Street 13Ca 13Ba 5Cc
Bishopsgate Street, Without 5Cc 5Cb
Bisset's Court, Wapping 15Ac
Bitt Alley, Turnmill Street 4Bb
Black Bear Inn, Piccadilly 10Bb 10Cb

Black Bell Alley, Petticoat Lane 6Ac
Black Bird Alley, Spicer Street 6Bb
Black Boy Alley, Chick Lane 4Bc
Black Boy Alley, in the Minories 14Aa
Black Boy Alley, Salt Petre Bank 14Bb
Black Boy Alley, Thames Street 12Ca
Black Bull Inn, Bishopsgate Street 5Cc
Black Bull Inn, Holbourn 4Ac
Black Bull Inn, Whitechapel 14Aa
Black Bull Yard, Whitechapel 14Aa
Black Dog Alley, Bowling Alley 19Aa
Black Dog Alley, East Smithfield 14Bb
Black Dog Yard, Shoreditch 5Cb
Black Dog Yard, near Vaux Hall 19Bc
Black Eagle Street, Brick Lane, Spitlefields 6Ab 6Bb
Black Eagle Yard, Black Eagle Street 6Ab 6Bb
Black Horse Alley, Barbican 4Cb 4Cc
Black Horse Alley, Fleet Street 12Ba
Black Horse Court, Aldersgate Street 4Cc
Black Horse Inn, Bishopsgate Street 5Cc
Black Horse Yard, Harrow Alley, Petticoat Lane 6Ac
Black Horse Yard, Nightingale Lane 14Bb
Black Horse Yard, Petticoat Lane 6Ac
Black Horse Yard, Pickax Street 4Cb
Black Horse Yard, Tottenham Court Road 2Cc
Black Horse Yard, Whitechapel 14Aa
Black Jack Alley, East Smithfield 14Bb
Black Lion Stairs, near York Buildings 11Bb
Black Lion Yard, Stoney Lane, Petticoat Lane 6Ac
Black Lion Yard, Whitechapel 6Bc
Black Moor Head Yard, York Street, St. James's Square 10Bb
Black Moor Street, Drury Lane 11Ba
Black Raven Alley, Thames Street 13Bb
Black Raven Court, Chiswell Street 5Ab
Black Raven Court, Golden Lane 5Ab
Black Raven Court, Leadenhall Street 13Ca
Black Raven Court, St. Olave's Street 13Cc
Black Raven Court, Seething Lane 13Cb
Black Raven Passage, Fetter Lane 4Ac
Black Spread Eagle Court, Blackman Street 13Ac
Black Swan Alley, in the Borough 13Bb
Black Swan Alley, Corbet's Court, Eagle Street 6Ab
Black Swan Alley, London Wall 5Cc
Black Swan Alley, Thames Street 13Aa 13Ab
Black Swan Court, Cannon Street 13Ba

Black Swan Court, Golden Lane 5Ab
Black Swan Court, Market Street 10Cb
Black Swan Court, in the Maze 13Bc
Black Swan Court, St. Paul's Church Yard 12Ca
Black Swan Court, Tower Street 13Cb
Black Swan Inn, Holbourn 4Ac
Black Swan Yard, Brown's Lane 6Ab
Black Swan Yard, Newington Buts 20Cb
Black and White Court, Old Bailey 12Ba
Blackbun's Alley, Rotherhith 14Bc
Blackburn's Mewse, Grosvenor Street 9Ba
Blackfriers, Ludgate 12Ba
Blackfriers Stairs, Water Street 12Ba
Blackman Street, Southwark 13Ac 20Ca
Blackmary's Hole 3Ca
Blackmoor Alley, Green Bank 15Ac
Blacksmiths' Hall, Lambeth Hill 12Ca
Blackwell Hall, Basinghall Street 5Ac
Blackwell Hall Court, First Postern, London Wall 5Ac
Bland Court, Narrow Street 16Ab
Bleeding Heart Yard, Cross Street, Hatton Garden 4Ac
Blenheim Street, Between Oxford Street and Great Marlborough Street 10Ba 2Bc
Blewit's Court, Fetter Lane 4Ac
Blind Beggar's Alley, Cow Cross 4Bc
Bloomsbury Market, Bloomsbury 3Ac 3Bc
Bloomsbury Square, Bloomsbury 3Bc 3Ac
Blossoms Inn, Laurence Lane 13Aa
Blossoms Street, White Lion Yard 6Ab
Blow Bladder Street, Cheapside 12Ca
Bludworth's Dock, Wapping 15Bb
Blue Anchor 22Cb
Blue Anchor Alley, Barnaby Street 13Cc
Blue Anchor Alley, Brook Street 15Ca
Blue Anchor Alley, Bunhill Row 5Ab
Blue Anchor Road 22Bb 22Cb
Blue Anchor Yard, Green Bank, near Morgan's Lane 13Cc
Blue Anchor Yard, Little Tower Hill 14Ab
Blue Anchor Yard, London Wall 5Ac
Blue Anchor Yard, Petty France, Westminster 18Ba 18Ca
Blue Anchor Yard, Rosemary Lane 14Bb 14Ba
Blue Ball Alley, in the Mint 12Cc
Blue Ball Alley, Saffron Hill 4Ab
Blue Ball Court, Artichoke Lane 14Cb
Blue Ball Court, Salisbury Square 12Ba

Blue Bell Yard, Dirty Lane 11Aa 11Ba
Blue Bell Yard, Petty France, Westminster 18Ca
Blue Boar Alley, White Street 13Ac
Blue Boar Court, Chick Lane 4Bc
Blue Boar Court, Friday Street 13Aa
Blue Boar Court, Rosemary Lane 14Aa
Blue Boar Inn, Whitechapel 14Aa
Blue Boar's Head Alley, Barbican 4Cb
Blue Boar's Head Inn, King Street, Westminster 11Ac
Blue Cross Street, Hedge Lane 10Cb
Blue Hart Court, Little Bell Alley, London Wall 5Bc
Blue Maid Alley, in the Borough 13Ac
Bluecoat School, Chapel Street, Westminster 18Ba
Bluegate Field, Ratcliff Highway 15Aa
Blunderbuss Alley, St. Thomas Apostles 13Aa
Boarded Entry, Crutchedfriers 14Aa
Boarded Entry, London Wall 5Bc
Boar's Head Court, Fleet Street 12Aa
Boar's Head Court, Grub Street 5Ab
Boar's Head Inn, Counter Lane, Southwark 13Ac
Boars Head Yard, Petticoat Lane 6Ac
Boddy's Bridge Yard, Upper Ground 12Ab
Bolt Court, in Fleet Street 12Aa
Bolt and Tun Alley, Strand 11Ba 11Bb
Bolt and Tun Court, Fleet Street 12Aa
Bolton Street, Hide Park Road 10Ab
Bond Stables, Rolls Building, Fetter Lane 4Ac
Bond Stables Yard, near Fetter lane 4Ac
Bond's Court, Walbrook 13Aa
Booker's Gardens, Leadenhall Street 13Ca
Boot Alley, Abchurch Lane 13Ba
Boot Alley, Kent Street 13Ac
Boot Passage, Piccadilly 10Bb
Booth Street, Brick Lane, Spittlefields 6Bc
Borough, Southwark 13Ac 13Bb
Borough Street, Southwark 13Ac 13Bb
Boss Alley, Shad Thames 14Ac
Boss Alley, Thames Street 13Cb
Boss Alley, near Trig Stairs, Thames Street 12Ca
Boss Court, near Lambeth Hill, Thames Street 12Ca
Bostwick Street, Old Gravel Lane 15Ab
Bosville Court, Devonshire Street 3Bb
Botolph Alley, Botolph Lane 13Ba
Botolph Lane, Thames Street 13Bb 13Ba
Botolph Wharf, Thames Street 13Bb

Bottle Alley, Bishopsgate Street 5Cc
Bottle of Hay Yard, Islington Road 4Bb
Boulton Street, Hide Park Road 10Ab
Bow Church Yard, Cheapside 13Aa
Bow Lane, Cheapside 13Ba
Bow Road, beyond the World's End 8Bc 8Bb 8Cb
Bow Street, Russell Street, Covent Garden 11Ba
Bow Street, St. Giles's Broad Street 3Ac
Bowl Court, Shoreditch 5Cb
Bowl Yard, St. Giles's Broadway 3Ac
Bowling Alley, Dean's Yard, Westminster 19Aa
Bowling Alley, Tenter Alley, Tooley Street 13Bc
Bowling Alley, Turnmill Street 4Bb
Bowling Alley, Whitecross Street 5Ab
Bowling Green Alley, Hoxton 5Ca
Bowling Green, Bandy Leg Walk 12Cc
Bowling Green, near Hospital Walk 5Ca
Bowling Green, near Hoxton Square 5Ca
Bowling Green Passage, Queen Street 12Cc
Bowling Green, Queen Street, Southwark 12Cc
Bowman's Court, Gardiner's Lane 11Ac
Bowyer's Court, Fenchurch Street 13Ca
Box Alley, Wapping Wall 15Bb
Boxwood Court, New Street Square 4Ac
Boyle's Head Court, in the Strand 11Ba
Brabant Court, Philpot Lane 13Ba
Brackley Street, Golden Lane 5Ab
Bradley's Alley, Queen Street 12Cc
Bradshaw's Rents, Portpool Lane 4Ab
Braze's Bridge, St. Olave Street 13Cc
Bread Street, Cheapside 13Aa
Bread Street Hill, Thames Street 12Ca
Breeze Hill, Radcliff Highway 14Cb
Breme's Buildings, Chancery Lane 4Ac
Brewer's Court, Basinghall Street 5Ac
Brewer's Court, Oxford Street 2Cc
Brewer's Court, St. Thomas Street 13Bc
Brewer's Hall, in Addle Street 5Ac
Brewers Key, Thames Street 13Cb
Brewers Lane, Thames Street 13Aa
Brewers Street, Bow Street, St. Giles's 3Ac
Brewers Street, near Golden Square 10Ba
Brewers Yard, Gilt Spur Street 4Bc 4Cc
Brewers Yard, Holywell Lane 5Cb
Brewers Yard, Saffron Hill 4Ab

Brewers Yard, Shoe Lane 4Bc
Brewers Yard, in the Strand 11Ab
Brewhouse Lane, Wapping Dock 15Ac
Brewhouse Yard, Chick Lane, near Saffron Hill 4Bc
Brewhouse Yard, at the Hermitage 14Bb
Brewhouse Yard, near Pillory Lane, St. Catharine's 14Bb
Brewhouse Yard, Turnmill Street 4Bb
Brewhouse Yard, Wapping 15Ac
Brewhouse Yard, Whitechapel 6Ac
Briant Alley, Briant Street, Shoreditch 6Ab
Briant Court, Briant Street, Shoreditch 6Ab
Briant Street, Shoreditch 6Ab
Brick Court, Middle Temple 12Aa
Brick Lane, Old Street 4Ca 4Cb
Brick Lane, Spittle Fields and White Chapel 6Bb 6Bc
Brick Street, Tyburn Lane 9Cb 9Cc
Brickhill Lane, Thames Street 13Aa
Brickinton Court, Coleman Street 5Bc
Bricklayers' Hall, Leadenhall Street 13Ca
Bricklayers Yard, Millbank 19Aa
Bride Court, Fleet Street 12Aa
Bride Lane, Fleet Street 12Ba
Bridewell, Clerkenwell 4Bb 4Ab
Bridewell, Fleetditch 12Ba
Bridewell, Tothill Fields, Westminster 18Ba
Bridewell Alley, Borough 13Ac
Bridewell Chapel and Burying Ground, Fleet Ditch 12Ba
Bridewell Walk, Clerkenwell 4Aa 4Ab
Bridge House, near the Bridge Yard 13Bb
Bridge Street, Westminster 11Ac
Bridge Yard, Tooly Street 13Bb
Bridges Street, Russel Street 11Ba
Bridgwater Square, Barbican 4Cb
Bridgwater Street, Bridgwater Square 4Cb
Bridle Lane, Brewers Street 10Ba
Brimstone Court, Church Yard Alley 14Bb
Bristol Street, Puddle Dock 12Ba
Brites Alley, St. Swithin's Lane 13Ba
Briton's Alley, Freeman's Lane 14Ba
Britt's Court, Nightingale Lane 14Bb
Broad Arrow Court, Grub Street 5Ab
Broad Bridge, Shadwell 15Cb
Broad Court, Duke's Place 13Ca
Broad Place, Broad St. Giles 3Ac
Broad Place, Flower and Dean Street 6Ac

Broad Place, King Street 13Ca
Broad St. Giles 3Ac
Broad St. Giles's Alms Houses 3Ac
Broad Sanctuary, Westminster 11Ac 19Aa
Broad Street, London Wall 5Bc 5Cc 13Ba
Broad Street, near Old Gravel Lane 15Ab
Broad Street, Poland Street 10Ba
Broad Street, Ratcliff Cross 15Ca 8Aa
Broad Street Buildings, Moorfields Quarters 5Cc
Broad Street Mewse, New Broad Street 5Cc 5Bc
Broad Wall, near the Upper Ground 12Ab 12Bb
Broad Way, Half Moon Alley, Bishopsgate Street 5Cc
Broad Way, Tothill Street 18Ca
Broad Yard, Crow Alley, Whitecross Street 5Ab
Broad Yard, Dirty Lane, Blackman Street 20Ca
Broad Yard, Milk Yard, near Wapping 15Bb
Broad Yard, St. John's Street 4Bb
Broad Yard, Swan Alley, near Golden Lane 4Cb 5Ab
Broken Wharf, Thames Street 12Ca
Brook Alley, Rotten Row 4Cb
Brook Street, Grosvenor Square 9Ca 10Aa
Brook Street, Holbourn 4Ac
Brook Street, near Ratcliff Square 15Ca 16Aa
Brook's Alley, Noble Street 4Cc
Brooks Market, Holbourn 4Ac
Brooks' Mewse, Avery Row, Brooks Street 9Ca 10Aa
Brooks Wharf, near Queenhithe 12Ca
Brook's Yard, Fore Street, Lambeth 19Bb
Broom Yard, Kent Street 21Aa
Broomstick Alley, Whitecross Street 5Ab
Brown Court, Chequer Alley, Brown Street 5Ab
Brownlow Street, Drury Lane 11Aa 11Ba
Brown's Buildings, High Holbourn 3Cc
Brown's Buildings, St. Mary Ax 13Ca
Brown's Court, Angel Alley, Bishopsgate Street 5Cc 5Cb
Brown's Court, near King and Queen Stairs, Rotherhithe 15Cb
Brown's Court, Little Old Bailey 4Bc
Brown's Court, Marlborough or Carnaby Market 10Ba
Brown's Court, Minories 14Aa
Brown's Court, Shoe Lane 4Ac
Brown's Gardens, Monmouth Street 11Aa
Brown's Lane, Wellin Street, Spittle Fields 6Ab 6Bb
Browns Passage, Green Street 9Ba
Brown's Street, Bunhill Fields 5Ab
Brown's Street, Duke Street, Grosvenor Square 9Ca 9Ba

Brown's Yard, in the Curtain, near Holywell Lane 5Cb
Brown's Wharf, St. Catharine's 14Bb
Brownson's Court, Ayliff Street 14Ba
Brunswick Court, Crucifix Lane 13Cc
Brunswick Court, Queen's Square 3Ab
Brush Court, East Smithfield 14Ab
Brush Yard, Kent Street 21Aa
Bruton Mewse, Bruton Street 10Aa 10Ab
Bruton Street, New Bond Street 10Aa
Buckeridge Street, Dyot Street 2Cc 3Ac
Buckingham Court, Charing Cross 11Ab
Buckingham House, St. James's Park 10Ac
Buckingham Street, in the Strand 11Ab
Buckle Street, Red Lion Street 14Ba
Bucklersbury, Cheapside 13Aa
Buck's Head Court, Great Distaff Lane 12Ca
Budge Row, Walbrook 13Aa
Bufford's Buildings, St. John Street 4Bb
Bull Alley, Broad Street 5Bc
Bull Alley, Bull Stairs 12Ab
Bull Alley, Fore Street, Lambeth 19Bb
Bull Alley, Kent Street 13Ac
Bull Alley, Whitechapel 6Bc
Bull Court, Dunning's Alley, Bishopsgate Street 5Cc
Bull Court, Petticoat Lane 6Ac
Bull Court, Ragged Row 4Cb
Bull Head Alley, Saffron Hill 4Ab
Bull Head Court, Cow Lane 4Bc
Bull Head Court, Jewin Street 5Ac
Bull Head Court, Newgate Street 4Cc
Bull Head Court, Wood Street 5Ac
Bull Head Yard, near Blackman Street 20Ca
Bull Inn Court, in the Strand 11Ba 11Bb
Bull Inn, High Holbourn 3Bc
Bull Inn, Kent Street 21Ba
Bull Inn, Leadenhall Street 13Ca
Bull Inn, Windmill Hill 4Ab
Bull Lane, Stepney 8Ac
Bull and Mouth Inn, Bull and Mouth Street, Aldersgate 4Cc
Bull and Mouth Street, St. Martin's le Grand 4Cc
Bull Stairs, Bull Alley, Upper Ground 12Ab 12Bb
Bull Yard, Goswell Street 4Cb
Bull Yard, Kingsland Road, Shoreditch 5Ca
Bullocks Court, Minories 14Aa
Bull's Court, Nightingale Lane, Limehouse 16Bb

Bunches Alley, Thrall Street 6Bc
Bunhill Court, Brown Street 5Ab
Bunhill Row, Bunhill Fields 5Ab
Bur Street, St. Catharine's Lane, and Nightingale Lane 14Bb
Burleigh Street, in the Strand 11Ba
Burlington House, Piccadilly 10Bb
Burlington Mewse, Great Swallow Street 10Aa 10Ba
Burlington Street, near New Bond Street 10Aa
Bury Street, near St. James' Street 10Bb
Bury Street, near St. Mary Axe 13Ca
Burying Ground, Bridewell Walk 4Ab
Burying Ground, Charterhouse 4Cb 4Bb
Burying Ground, Church Lane, Rotherhithe 15Bc
Burying Ground, Ewers Street Park, for Quakers 12Cc
Burying Ground, Grey Fryers 4Cc
Burying Ground, Kent Street 21Ba 21Bb
Burying Ground, Royal Row 5Bb 5Ab
Burying Ground, Whitechapel 6Cc
Burying Ground, Worcester Street 13Ac
Bush Lane, Canon Street 13Aa 13Ba
Bushel's Rents, Wapping 14Bc
Bushie's Rents, St. John's Court, Cow Lane 4Bc
Butcher Row, East Smithfield 14Bb
Butcher Row, Ratcliff 16Aa
Butcher Row, Temple Bar 11Ca
Butcherhall Lane, Newgate Street 4Cc
Butcher's Alley, St. John Street 4Bb
Butchers' Hall, Pudding Lane 13Ba
Butcher's Yard, Brick Lane 4Ca
Butler's Alley, Grub Street 5Ac
Butler's Alley, Little Moorfields 5Bc
Butler's Alley, Windmill Hill Row 5Bb
Butler's Alms Houses, Chapel Street, Westminster 18Ba
Butlers Court, Houndsditch 5Cc
Buttermilk Alley, Phœnix Street 6Ab

Cabbage Alley, Long Lane 21Ba
Cabbage Lane, near King's Arms Stairs 11Bc 11Cc
Cable Street, Ragfair, near Well Close Square 14Ca 14Ba
Calender Court, Drury Lane 3Ac 3Bc
Calender Court, Long Alley, Moorfields 5Cc
Camberwell Road, Newington Butts 20Cb
Cambridge Street, Broad Street 10Ba
Camden Court, Grub Street 5Ab
Camel Row, Mile End 7Bb

Camomile Court, Camomile Street 5Cc
Camomile Street, Bishopsgate Street 5Cc 13Ca
Campion Lane, Thames Street 13Ab
Canary Court, in the Strand 11Ba
Cane's Wharf, Milford Lane 11Ca
Cannon Alley, Pater-noster Row 12Ca
Cannon Street, Ratcliff Highway 15Aa 15Ab
Cannon Street, Walbrook 13Aa 13Ba
Canterbury Court, Blackfriars 12Ba
Canterbury Court, Phoenix Street 6Ab
Capt. Fishers Alms Houses 7Bb
Carey Street, Searle's Street, Lincoln's Inn Fields 11Ca 3Cc
Carlisle Street, Soho Square 10Ca
Carman's Yard, Park Gate, Southwark 13Ac
Carnaby, or Marborough Market, Carnaby Street 10Ba
Carnaby Street, Silver Street 10Ba
Caroline Court, Saffron Hill 4Bc
Carpenters Buildings, London Wall 5Bc
Carpenters' Court, Aldermanbury 5Ac
Carpenters' Hall, London Wall 5Bc
Carpenters Street, Mount Row 9Ca
Carpenter's Yard, Beech Lane 5Ab
Carpenter's Yard, Blackman Street 13Ac
Carpenters Yard, Coleman Street 5Bc
Carpenters Yard, London Wall 5Bc
Carpenters Yard, Long Lane 4Cc
Carriers Street, Buckeridge Street 3Ac
Cart Yard, Harrow Alley, Whitechapel 14Aa
Cart Yard, White's Yard, Rosemary Lane 14Bb
Carter Court, Cursitor's Alley, Bristol Street 12Ba
Carteret Street, Broadway 18Ca
Carter's Rents, Brick Lane 6Bb
Carters Street, Cutler's Street, Houndsditch 5Cc
Carthusian Street, Pick Ax Street 4Cb
Cary Lane, Foster Lane 4Cc
Castle Alley, Cornhill 13Ba
Castle Court, Birchin Lane 13Ba
Castle Court, Budge Row 13Aa
Castle Court, Castle Alley, Castle Street 13Ab
Castle Court, Castle Street 11Aa
Castle Court, College Hill 13Aa
Castle Court, Laurence Lane 13Aa
Castle Court, St. Martin's Lane 11Aa
Castle Court, in the Strand 11Ab
Castle Court, Whitecross Street 5Ac

Castle and Falcon Inn, Aldersgate 4Cc
Castle Inn, near Windmill Hill 5Bb
Castle Inn, in Wood Street 5Ac
Castle Lane, Castle Street, Southwark 13Ab
Castle Lane, James Street, Westminster 18Ba
Castle Lane, Thames Street 12Ca
Castle Street, Air Street 10Bb
Castle Street, near Austin Street, Hackney Road 6Aa
Castle Street, Hart Street 3Ac
Castle Street, near Long Acre 11Aa
Castle Street, Oxford Market 2Ac
Castle Street, Red Cross Street, in the Park 13Ac
Castle Street, near the Royal Mewse 11Aa 11Ab
Castle Street, Thames Street 12Ca
Castle Yard, Bevis Mark 13Ca
Castle Yard, near the Broadway 18Ca
Castle Yard, Hermitage Bridge 14Bb
Castle Yard, Holbourn 4Ac
Castle Yard, Houndsditch 5Cc
Castle Yard, Kingsland Road, Shoreditch 5Ca
Castle Yard, Piccadilly 10Bb
Castle Yard, Saffron Hill 4Ab 4Bb
Cat Alley, Long Lane 4Cc 4Cb
Cateaton Street, Aldermanbury 13Aa 5Ac
Catharine Court, Princes Street 13Ba
Catharine Court, Seething Lane 13Cb
Catharine Street, in the Strand 11Ba
Catharine Wheel Alley, Petticoat Lane 5Cc
Catharine Wheel Alley, Snow Hill 4Bc
Catharine Wheel Alley, Whitechapel 6Ac 6Bc
Catharine Wheel Court, Catharine Wheel Alley, Whitechapel 6Bc
Catharine Wheel Inn, Bishopsgate Street 5Cc
Catharine Wheel Inn, Borough 13Ac
Catharine Wheel Yard, Blackman Street 13Ac
Catharine Wheel Yard, London Wall 5Ac
Catharine Wheel Yard, St. James's Street 10Bb
Catharine Wheel Yard, West Smithfield 4Bc
Catlin Alley, Shoreditch 6Ab
Cats Head Court, Orchard Street 18Ca
Cat's Hole, Tower Ditch, near Iron Gate 14Ab
Cavendish Square, near Oxford Street 2Ac
Cavendish Street, Oxford Street 2Ac
Cecil Court, St. Martin's Lane 11Aa
Cecil Street, in the Strand 11Bb 11Ba

Chain Gate, near St. Saviour's Church, Southwark 13Bb
Chamberlain's Wharf, near the Bridge Yard 13Bb
Chambers Street, near Prescot Street, Goodman's Fields 14Ba
Chambers Street, Upper Shadwell 15Ba 15Ab
Chancery Lane, Fleet Street 3Cc 4Ac
Chandler's Rents, near Addle Hill 12Ca
Chandler's Street, Dukes Street 9Ca
Chandos Street, Covent Garden 11Ab 11Aa
Channell Row, near Bridge Street 11Ac
Chapel Alley, King Street, Oxford Street 10Ba
Chapel Alley, Long Acre 11Aa
Chapel Court, Henrietta Street 1Cc
Chapel Court, South Audley Street 9Cb
Chapel Street, Audley Street 9Bb
Chapel Street, Red Lion Street 3Bb 3Cb
Chapel Street, Westminster 18Ba 18Ca
Chapter House Court, St. Paul's Church Yard 12Ca
Chapter House, St. Paul's Church Yard 12Ca
Charing Cross 11Ab
Charles Court, St. Martin's Lane 11Ab
Charles Court, in the Strand 11Ab
Charles Square, Charles's Street, Hoxton 5Ba
Charles Street, Bridgwater Gardens 4Cb
Charles Street, Grosvenor Square 9Ca
Charles Street, Hatton Garden 4Ab
Charles Street, Old Gravel Lane 15Ab
Charles Street, Oxford Street 2Cc
Charles Street, Petfield Street, Hoxton 5Ba
Charles Street, Russell Street 11Ba
Charles Street, St. James's Square 10Cb
Charles Street, Westminster 11Ac
Charter House, or Sutton Hospital, near Long Lane 4Cb 1Bb
Charterhouse Lane, Charterhouse Square 4Bc 4Cb 4Bb
Charterhouse Square, near West Smithfield 4Cb
Charterhouse Street, Long Lane 4Cc 4Cb
Cheapside 13Aa
Chelsea Bridge, Chelsea 17Cb
Chelsea College 17Ac 17Bc
Chelsea College Burying Ground 17Bc
Chelsea Road 17Cb 18Aa 18Ab
Chelsea Road, Pemblico, or the King's Road 17Ab 17Bb 17Ca 17Ba
Chelsea Water-works 17Cc
Chelton's Court, Bedfordbury 11Ab
Chequer Alley, in the Borough 13Bb

Chequer Alley, Whitecross Street 5Ab
Chequer Court, Charing Cross 11Ab
Chequer Court, St. Catharine's Lane 14Ab 14Bb
Chequer Inn, Dowgate Hill 13Aa
Chequer Inn, Holbourn 4Ac
Chequer Yard, Dowgate Hill 13Aa
Chequer Yard, Whitechapel 14Aa
Cherry Garden Stairs, Rotherhithe 14Cc
Cherry Garden Street, Rotherhithe 22Ca 23Aa 14Cc
Cherry Tree Alley, Golden Lane 4Cb
Cherry Tree Alley, Whitecross Street 5Ab
Cherry Tree Court, Aldersgate Street 4Cc
Cherry Tree Court, Gardiner's Lane 11Ac
Cherry Tree Court, Piccadilly 10Bb
Cherubin Court, White's Alley 14Ba
Chesterfield House, Curzon Street 9Cb
Chesters Key, Thames Street 13Cb
Cheves's Court, Nightingale Lane, Limehouse 16Bb
Chichester Rents, Chancery Lane 3Cc 4Ac
Chick Lane, West Smithfield 4Bc
Chidlies Court, Pall Mall 10Cb
Chigwell Hill, Radcliff Highway 15Ab
Child's Court, in the Strand 11Bb
Chiswell Street, Whitecross Street 5Ab 5Bb
Chitterling Alley, Beer Lane 13Cb
Christ Church, Green Walk and Bennet Street 12Bb
Christ Church Hospital, Newgate Street 4Cc
Christ Church, Newgate Street 4Cc
Christ Church, in Spitlefields 6Ac 6Bc
Christopher Inn, Barnaby Street 13Cc
Christopher's Alley, in the Borough 13Ac
Christopher's Alley, Lambert Street 14Ba
Christopher's Alley, St. Martin's le Grand 4Cc
Christopher's Alley, Threadneedle Street 13Ba
Christopher's Alley, Upper Moorfields 5Bb 5Cb
Christopher's Court, Cartwright Street,
and Rosemary's Lane 14Ba
Church Alley, Basinghall Street 5Ac
Church Alley, New Rents, Compter Street 13Ab 13Bb
Church Alley, Old Jewry 13Aa
Church Alley, Puddle-dock Hill 12Ba
Church Alley, St. Mary Hill 13Ca 13Cb
Church Alley, Thames Street 12Ca
Church Alley, Watling Street, near Old Change 12Ca
Church Alley, Whitechapel 6Bc

Church Court, Church Passage, Piccadilly 10Bb
Church Court, St. Clement's Lane 13Ba
Church Court, in the Strand 11Ab
Church Entry, Shoemakers Row, Blackfriers 12Ba
Church Hill, Puddle Dock Hill 12Ba
Church Lane, Cable Street 14Ba 14Ca
Church Lane, Church Street, Dyet Street 2Cc 3Ac
Church Lane, Elephant Lane, Rotherith 15Bc
Church Lane, Houndsditch 14Aa
Church Lane, Newington Butts 20Cb
Church Lane, Ropewalk, Limehouse 16Cb
Church Lane, in the Strand 11Ab
Church Lane, Thames Street 13Ac 13Ab
Church Lane, White Street, Southwark 13Ac
Church Lane, Whitechapel 6Bc
Church Passage, Piccadilly 10Bb
Church Row, Whitechapel 14Aa
Church Stairs, near Jamaica Street, Rotherhithe 15Bc
Church Street, Baynbridge Street 3Ac
Church Street, Dyot Street, Broad St. Giles's 3Ac
Church Street, Lambeth 19Bb
Church Street, Millbank 19Aa
Church Street, Shoreditch Fields 6Ba
Church Street, Soho 10Ca
Church Street, Spittlefields 6Ac 6Bc
Church Yard Alley, Fetter Lane 4Ac
Church Yard Alley, Hole Stairs 13Bb
Church Yard Alley, Rosemary Lane 14Bb
Church Yard Alley, Thames Street 13Bb
Church Yard Alley, Tooly Street 13Bb
Church Yard Court, Inner Temple Lane 12Aa
Church Yard, Fetter Lane 4Ac
Chymisters Alley, Bedfordbury 11Aa
Cinnamon Street, near Old Gravel Lane 15Ac 15Bb
Clare Court, Drury Lane 11Ba
Clare Market, Vere Street 11Ca
Clare Street, Clare Market 11Ca
Clarges Street, Hide Park Road 10Ab
Clark's Alley, Bishopsgate Street 5Cc
Clarks' Hall, Wood Street 5Ac
Clark's Orchard, Rotherhithe Wall 15Ac 23Bc
Clement's Court, Milk Street 5Ac
Clement's Inn, by St. Clement Danes Church 11Ca
Clerkenwell Close, Clerkenwell 4Bb 4Ab
Clerkenwell Green, Clerkenwell 4Cc

Clerkenwell School, Aylesbury Street 4Bb
Cleveland Court, Cleveland Row, St. James's 10Bc
Cleveland Court, St. James's Place 10Bb
Cleveland Row, St. James's 10Bc
Cleveland Street, St. James's Palace 10Bc
Cleveland Yard, King Street, St. James's Square 10Bb
Clifford Street, New Bond Street 10Aa
Clifford's Inn Lane, Fleet Street 12Aa
Clifford's Inn, by St. Dunstan's Church 12Aa
Clink Street, near Deadman's Place 13Ab
Clink Yard, Clink Street 13Ab
Cloak Lane, Dowgate Hill 13Aa
Clock and Wheatsheaf Court, Houndsditch 14Aa
Cloister Court, Glass House Yard, Water Lane 12Ba
Cloister Court, Inner Temple 12Aa
Cloisters, Great and Little, Westminster Abbey 19Aa
Cloisters, Queen's Court, St. Catherine's 14Bb 14Cb
Cloth Fair, West Smithfield 4Bb
Clothworkers' Hall, Mincing Lane 13Ca
Club Row, New Cock Lane 6Ab
Coach and Horses Yard, Aldersgate Street 4Cc
Coach and Horses Yard, Coleman Street 5Bc
Coach and Horses Yard, Fans Alley 4Cb
Coach and Horses Yard, Oxford Street 2Bc
Coach and Horses Yard, St. John's Court 4Bb
Coach and Horses Yard, Wood Street 5Ac
Coachmakers' Hall, Noble Street 4Cc
Coal Stairs, near Gold's Hill, Lower Shadwell 15Cb
Coal Wharf 14Ab
Coal Yard, Goswell Street 4Ca 4Cb
Coal Yard, High Holbourn 3Bc
Coal Yard, Willow Street 12Cb
Coalman's Alley, Puddle Dock 12Ba
Coats' Farm, Coats's Lane 6Ca
Coat's Lane, near Bithnal Green 6Ca
Cobb's Court, Blackfriers 12Ba
Cobbs Yard, Pettycoat Lane 6Ac
Cock Alley, Deadman's Place 13Ab
Cock Alley, East Smithfield 14Bb
Cock Alley, Ludgate Street 12Ba
Cock Alley, Moor Lane 5Ac
Cock Alley, Norton Falgate 5Cb
Cock Alley, near Pepper Alley, in the Borough 13Bb
Cock Alley, Portpool Lane 4Ab
Cock Alley, Shoreditch 6Ab

Cock Alley, Turnmill Street 4Bb
Cock Alley, Wapping 14Cc
Cock Alley, Whitechapel 6Bc
Cock Alley Stairs, near Pepper Alley Stairs 13Bb
Cock Court, Grub Street 5Ab
Cock Court, Ludgate Hill 12Ba
Cock Court, New Street, Broad Street 10Ba
Cock Court, Philip Lane 5Ac
Cock Court, Poor Jewry Lane 14Aa
Cock Court, St. Martin's le Grand 4Cc
Cock Hill, Anchor Street 6Ab
Cock Hill, Upper Shadwell 15Cb
Cock Inn, Old Street 4Cb
Cock Inn, Pickaxe Street 4Cb
Cock Lane, near Shoreditch 6Aa
Cock Lane, Snow Hill 4Bc
Cock Yard, near Angel Alley, Bishopsgate Street 5Cc
Cock Yard, Bennet Street, Westminster 10Cc
Cock Yard, Bishopsgate Street 5Cc
Cock Yard, East Smithfield 14Bb
Cock Yard, Haymarket 10Cb
Cock Yard, Tuthill Street 18Ca
Cock and Hoop Yard, Houndsditch 6Ac
Cocket Alley, Fore Street, Lambeth 19Bb
Cockpit Court, Gravel Lane 12Bb
Cockpit Court, Great Wild Street 11Ba
Cockpit Court, Jewin Street 4Cc
Cockpit Court, King's Way, near Bedford Row 3Cb
Cockpit Court, Shoe Lane 4Ac 4Bc
Cockpit, Whitehall 11Ac
Cockpit Yard, Denin's Passage, James Street 3Cb
Cocks Head Court, Golden Lane 5Ab
Cockspur Street, Pallmall 10Cb
Coffee House Alley, Thames Street 13Aa
Coffins Court, St. Dunstan's Hill 13Cb
Cogdell Court, near Pultney Street 10Ba
Colchester Street, Red Lion Street 6Bc
Colchester Street, Woodrofe Lane 14Aa
Cold Bath, Cold Bath Square 4Ab
Cold Bath Row, Cold Bath Street 4Ab
Cold Bath, St. Mary le Bone 1Cc
Cold Bath Square, Cold Bath Fields 4Ab
Cole Harbour Lane, Thames Street 13Ab 13Bb
Cole Harbour Stairs, Cole Harbour, Thames Street 13Ab
Cole Harbour, Thames Street 13Bb

Coleman Alley, Brown Street 5Ab
Coleman Street, Lothbury 5Ac 5Bc 13Ba
Coleman Street, New Gravel Lane 15Bb
Coleman's Yard, Barnaby Street 21Ca
Coles Alley, Whitechapel 6Bc
College Alm's Houses, College Yard, Deadman's Place 13Ac
College Court, Cowcross 4Bc
College Court, Nightingale Lane 14Bb 14Cb
College Court, Stable Yard, Dean's Yard 19Aa
College Hill, Thames Street 13Aa
College Street, Narrow Wall, Lambeth 11Cc 11Bc
College Street, Westminster 19Aa
College Yard, Deadman's Place 13Ac
Collier's Rents, White Street 13Ac
Collingwood Street, Maze Pond 13Bc
Collin's Court, Brick Street 9Cc
Collin's Court, Farmer Street 15Bb
Colson's Court, Drury Lane 11Ba
Common Lane, Thames Street, near Puddle Dock 12Ba
Compton Street, St. John's Street 4Ba 4Ca 4Bb
Compton Street, Soho 10Ca
Conduit Close, Phoenix Street 6Ab
Conduit Court, Long Acre 11Aa
Conduit Street Chapel 10Aa
Conduit Street, New Bond Street 10Aa
Constitution Hill 9Cc 10Ac
Cony Court, Grays Inn 3Cc 3Cb
Cooks' Alm's Houses, Essex Road 8Ba
Cook's Court, Camomile Street 5Cc
Cook's Court, Searle Street 11Ca 3Cc
Cooks' Hall, Aldersgate Street 4Cc
Cooper's Alley, Wapping Dock 15Ac
Cooper's Alley, Whitecross Street 5Ab
Coopers' Alm's Houses, Schoolhouse Lane 15Ca
Cooper's Court, East Smithfield 14Bb
Coopers' Hall, Basinghall Street 5Ac
Cooper's Yard, Brewhouse Lane, Wapping 15Ac
Cooper's Yard, Greenbank 13Cb
Cooper's Yard, Lower Shadwell 15Bb
Coppice Row, Hockley in the Hole 4Ab
Coppice Row Workhouse, Clerkenwell 4Ab
Copthall Court, Throgmorton Street 5Bc 13Ba
Coral Court, near Southampton Street, Strand 11Ba
Corbet's Court, Brown's Lane 6Ab
Corbet's Court, Gracechurch Street 13Ba

Cordwainers and Bread Street School, Well Court, Bow Lane 13Aa
Cordwainers' Hall, Great Distaff Lane 12Ca
Cork Street, Burlington Gardens 10Aa 10Ab
Corkcutters Alley, Long Ditch 18Ca
Corn Hill, Grace Church Street 13Ba
Corporation Lane, Bridewell Walk 4Ba 4Ab 4Aa
Counsellors Alley, Pearl Street 6Ab
Counter Alley, Borough 13Cb
Counter Alley, Poultry 13Aa
Counter Lane, St. Margaret's Hill 13Ac
Counting House Yard, Christ's Hospital 4Cc
Court of Requests 19Aa
Court Street, Whitechapel 7Ac
Cousen's Rents, White's Yard, Rosemary Lane 14Bb
Couzens Lane, Thames Street 13Ab 13Aa
Covent Garden Market 11Ba
Coventry Court, Coventry Street 10Cb
Coventry Street, Hay Market, near Leicester Fields 10Ca 10Cb
Cow Alley, Free-school Street 14Ac
Cow Court, Jamaica Street 15Bc
Cow Court, Old Street 4Cb
Cow Cross, near West Smithfield 4Bc 4Bb
Cow Lane, New Gravel Lane 15Bb
Cow Lane, Snow Hill 4Bc
Cow Lane, Trinity Street, Rotherhithe 16Bc
Cow Yard, Artichoke Lane 14Cb
Cowley Street, Westminster 19Aa
Cox's Alley, Leather Lane 4Ab
Cox's Court, Aldersgate Street 4Cc
Cox's Court, Kent Street 13Ac
Cox's Gardens, near Wapping 15Bb
Cox's Key, Thames Street 13Bb
Cox's Square, near Bell Lane, Spittlefields 6Ac
Cox's Wharf, near Battle Bridge 13Cb
Cox's Yard, Pennington Street 14Cb
Crabtree Lane, Castle Street 6Aa
Crabtree Orchard, Clare Market 11Ca
Cradle Court, Aldersgate Street 4Cc
Cradle Court, Cowcross 4Bc
Cradle Court, Fenchurch Street 13Ca
Cradle Court, Fore Street 5Ac 5Bc
Cradle Court, Redcross Street 5Ab
Cradle Court, St. Mary Ax 13Ca

Crag's Court, Charing Cross 11Ab
Cranbourn Alley, Leicester Fields 11Aa
Crane Court, Fleet Street 12Aa 4Ac
Crane Court, Lambert Hill, Thames Street 12Ca
Crane Court, Old Change 12Ca
Cranebourn Alley, Leicester Fields 11Aa
Craven Buildings, Drury Lane 11Ba 11Ca
Craven Mewse, Drury Lane 11Ba 11Ca
Craven Street, in the Strand 11Ab
Crawford's Court, Rosemary Lane 14Ba
Creechurch Lane, Leadenhall Street 13Ca
Creed Lane, Ludgate Street 12Ba 12Ca
Cripplegate Alm's Houses, 5Aa
Cripplegate, London Wall 5Ac
Crispin Street, Lamb Street, Spittlefields 6Ac 6Ab
Croft's Yard, Nightingale Lane, East Smithfield 14Bb
Cromwell's Palace, Charing Cross 11Ab
Crooked Billet Court, Long Alley, Moorfields 5Bc
Crooked Lane, Fish Street Hill 13Ba 13Bb
Crooked Lane, Mint Street 13Ac
Cropp's Yard, Back Lane, Lambeth 19Bb
Crosby Square, Bishopsgate Street 13Ca
Crosby Street, Free School Street 14Ac
Crosby Street, St. Mary Axe 13Ca
Cross Alley, Wall Alley, Wapping 15Ac 14Cc
Cross Court, Beaufort Buildings, Strand 11Ba
Cross Court, Carnaby Street 10Ba
Cross Court, Russel Court 11Ba
Cross Keys Alley, Barnaby Street 13Cc
Cross Keys Alley, Whitechapel 6Cc
Cross Keys Court, Little Britain 4Cc
Cross Keys Court, London Wall 5Bc
Cross Keys Court, Watling Street 13Aa
Cross Keys Court, Whitecross Street 5Ac
Cross Keys Inn, Barbican 4Cb
Cross Keys Inn, Gracechurch Street 13Ba
Cross Keys Inn, St. John's Street 4Bb
Cross Keys Inn, Wood Street 13Aa
Cross Keys Yard, Whitecross Street 5Ac
Cross Lane, Bush Lane 13Ba
Cross Lane, Long Acre 11Ba
Cross Lane, Parker's Lane, Drury Lane 3Bc
Cross Lane, St. Dunstan's Hill 13Cb
Cross Lane, St. Mary Hill 13Cb
Cross Lane, Shad Thames 14Ac

Cross Street, Hatton Garden 4Ac
Cross Street, King Street 10Ba
Cross Street, Marygold Street, Rotherhithe 22Ca
Crossby Square, Bishopsgate Street 13Ca
Cross'd Daggers Court, Grub Street 5Ab
Cross'd Guns Court, Rosemary Lane 14Ba
Crowder's Rents, Narrow Street, Ratcliff 16Aa 16Ab
Crowder's Well Alley, Jewin Street 4Cc
Crowder's Well, near Jewin Street 5Ac
Crown Alley, Broad St. Giles 3Ac
Crown Alley, Dorset Street 12Ba
Crown Alley, Petticoat Lane 6Ac
Crown Alley, Upper Moorfield 5Bb 5Cb 5Cc
Crown Alley, Whitecross Street 5Ab
Crown Court, Aldersgate Street 4Cc
Crown Court, Angel Hill 2Cc
Crown Court, Bankside 12Cb
Crown Court, Broadstreet 5Bc
Crown Court, Butcher Row 11Ca
Crown Court, Chancery Lane 12Aa
Crown Court, Cheapside 13Aa
Crown Court, Church Lane, Rag Fair 14Ba
Crown Court, Duke Street, Westminster 11Ac
Crown Court, Dunnings Alley, Bishopsgate Street 5Cc
Crown Court, East Smithfield 14Bb
Crown Court, French Alley 4Cb
Crown Court, Golden Lane 5Ab
Crown Court, Grace Church Street 13Ba
Crown Court, Grub Street 5Ab
Crown Court, King Street, Tooly Street 13Bc
Crown Court, near Knaves Acre 10Ca
Crown Court, Little Pearl Street 6Ab
Crown Court, Long Acre 11Aa
Crown Court, Narrow Wall 11Cb
Crown Court, New Gravel Lane 15Bb
Crown Court, Newington Butts 20Cb
Crown Court, Old Gravel Lane 15Ab
Crown Court, Pickle Herring Street 14Ac
Crown Court, Portpool Lane 4Ab
Crown Court, Quaker Street 6Ab
Crown Court, Russel Street 11Ba
Crown Court, St. Catharine's Lane and Tower Ditch 14Ab
Crown Court, Seething Lane 13Cb
Crown Court, Threadneedle Street 13Ba
Crown Court, Warwick Lane 4Cc

Crown Court, White Street 13Ac
Crown Court, Whitecross Street 5Ab
Crown Court, White's Alley, Coleman Street 5Bc
Crown Court, Worcester Street 13Ac
Crown and Cushion Court, West Smithfield Sheep Pens 4Bc
Crown Inn, Blackman Street 20Ca
Crown Inn, Holbourn 4Ac
Crown Office Row, in the Temple 12Aa
Crown and Sceptre Court, St. James's Street 10Bb
Crown and Sheers Court, Rosemary Lane 14Aa
Crown Street, Hoxton 5Ca
Crucifix Lane, Barnaby Street 13Cc
Crutched Friers, near Tower Hill 13Ca 14Aa
Cuckolds Point Stairs 16Bc
Cucumber Alley, Queen Street, Seven Dials 11Aa
Cullum Street, Fenchurch Street 13Ca
Culver Court, Fenchurch Street 13Ca
Cumber Court, Blackman Street 21Aa
Cumber's Court, Blackman Street 21Aa
Cupers Bridge 11Cb
Cupers Bridge Stairs 11Cb
Cupers Gardens 11Cb
Cupid's Alley, Golden Lane 5Ab
Curriers Alley, Bristol Street 12Ba
Curriers Alley, Shoe Lane 4Bc
Curriers Court, London Wall 5Ac
Curriers' Hall, London Wall 5Ac
Cursitors Alley, Chancery Lane 4Ac
Curtain, Hog Lane 5Cb
Curzon Street Chapel 9Cb
Curzon Street, Tiburn Lane 9Cb
Cushion Court, Pig Street 13Ba
Custom House Court, Beer Lane 13Cb
Custom House, Thames Street 13Cb
Custom House Key, Thames Street 13Cb
Custom House Stairs 13Cb
Cutlers' Hall, Cloak Lane 13Aa
Cutlers Street, Houndsditch 5Cc
Cut-throat Lane, Upper Shadwell 15Ca

Dacre's Street, New Tothill Street 18Ca
Dagger Court, Quaker Street 6Ab
Dagget's Court, Moorfields Quarters 5Cc 5Bc
Dagget's Farm, St. Mary le Bone 1Bb
Dancing Bridge, Pickle Herring Street 14Ac

Dancing Bridge Stairs 14Ac
Danes Church, Well Close Square 14Ca 14Cb
Darby Court, Channel Row, Westminster 11Ac
Darby Court, Piccadilly 10Bb
Dark Entry, Great St. Ann's Lane 18Ca
Dark Entry, Shoemaker Row, Aldgate 14Aa
Dark House Lane, Billingsgate 13Bb
Dark House Lane, Thames Street 12Ca
Dartmouth Street, Tothill Street 10Cc 18Ca
Dart's Alley, Whitechapel 6Bc
David Street, near Grosvenor's Square 9Ca
Davis's Coal Yard 12Cb
Dawson's Alley, St. Martin's Lane 11Ab
Deacon's Court, Quaker Street 6Ab
Deadman's Place, Southwark 13Ab
Dean Street, Cock Hill 15Cb
Dean Street, Fetter Lane 4Ac
Dean Street, High Holbourn 3Bc
Dean Street, Soho 10Ca
Dean Street, Thieving Lane, Westminster 11Ac
Dean Street, Tiburn Lane 9Cc
Dean's Court, Great Carter Lane 12Ca
Dean's Court, Little Old Bailey 4Bc
Dean's Court, St. Martin's le Grand 4Cc
Dean's Yard, near the Cloisters, Westminster 19Aa
Dean's Yard, Kingsland Road, Shoreditch 5Ca
Dearing's Rents, Liquor Pond Street 4Ab
Deford's Court, Broad Street, Marshal Street 10Ba
Delahay Street, Westminster 10Cc 11Ac
Denham's Yard, Drury Lane 19Ca 19Ba
Denmark Court, in the Strand 11Ba
Denmark Street, Ratcliff Highway 14Ca 14Cb
Denmark Street, St. Giles's 10Ca 2Cc 3Ac
Dennis's Passage, James Street 3Cb
Deptford Road, Rotherhithe 23Ba 23Bb
Derby Court, Channel Row, Westminster 11Ac
Derby Court, Piccadilly 10Bb
Devereux Court, in the Strand 11Ca
Devonshire Court, Pickax Street 4Cb
Devonshire House, Piccadilly 10Ab
Devonshire Square, Bishopsgate Street 5Cc
Devonshire Street, Bishopsgate Street 5Cc
Devonshire Street, Queen's Square 3Bb 3Bc
Diamond Court, Pearl Street 6Ab
Dickson's Alley, Long Lane 21Ca

Dirty Lane, Blackman Street 12Cc 20Ca 21Ca
Dirty Lane, Long Acre 11Ba
Dirty Lane, Shoreditch 6Ab
Dirty Lane, Stoney Street 13Ab
Dirty Lane, Strand 11Bb 11Ba
Distaff Lane, Old Change 12Ca
Distillers Yard, Great Tower Hill 14Ab
Distillers Yard, Shoreditch 5Ca
Ditch Side, Collingwood Street 13Bc
Dizzel's Court, Beach Lane 5Ab
Dobbins Alley 4Bb 4Ab
Dock Head, Hermitage 14Bb
Dock Head, St. Saviour's Dock 14Ac
Dock Side, Hermitage Dock 14Bb
Doctor Williams's Library, Red Cross Street 5Ac
Doctors Commons, Bennets Hill 12Ca
Doddington Street, Leather Lane 4Ac
Dog and Bear Yard, in the Borough 13Ac
Dog and Bear Yard, Crucifix Lane 13Cc
Dog and Duck Alley, New Bond Street 10Aa
Dog and Duck Stairs, near Deptford 24Cb
Dog Row, Mile End 7Aa 7Bb
Dog's Head and Pottage Pot Alley, Old Street 4Cb 4Ca
Dogwell Court, Lombard Street, Whitefriars 12Aa
Dolittle Alley, Little Carter Lane 12Ca
Dolphin Alley, Wapping 14Cc
Dolphin Court 5Ac
Dolphin Court, near Gun Street 6Ac
Dolphin Court, High Holbourn 3Cc
Dolphin Court, Little Distaff Lane 12Ca
Dolphin Court, Ludgate Hill 12Ba
Dolphin Court, Noble Street 4Cc
Dolphin Court, St. Catharine's Court 14Ab
Dolphin Inn, Bishopsgate Street 5Cc
Dolphin Inn, Smithfield 4Bc
Dolphin Yard, Blackman Street 13Ac
Dolphin Yard, Dean Street 10Ca
Dorset Court, Channel Row, Westminster 11Ac
Dorset Court, Dorset Street 12Ba
Dorset Stairs, Dorset Street 12Ba
Dorset Street, Red Lion Street 6Ac
Dorset Street, Salisbury Square, near Fleet Street 12Ba
Dove Court, Labour in Vain Hill, Thames Street 12Ca
Dove Court, Leather Lane 4Ab
Dove Court, Old Jewry 13Aa

Dove Court, St. Swithin's Lane 13Ba
Dove Court, Turnmill Street 4Bb
Dove Court, Water Lane 12Aa
Dover Court, Dover Street 10Ab
Dover Street, Piccadilly 10Ab
Dowgate Hill, Thames Street 13Aa
Dowgate Stairs, Cousen's Lane 13Ab
Dowgate Wharf, Thames Street 13Ab
Down Street, Hide Park Road 9Cc 9Cb
Downing Street, Westminster 11Ac
Drake Street, Red Lion Square 3Bc
Draper's Alley, Woodroffe Street, Tower Hill 14Aa
Drapers' Alms Houses, Blackman Street 20Ca
Draper's Court, Prince's Street 13Ba
Drapers' Hall, Throgmorton Street 13Ba
Drew's Court, Peter Street, Westminster 18Ca
Drift Way, near Bethnal Green 7Ba 7Ca
Drivers Yard, Old Street 5Ab
Drum Alley, Drury Lane 11Ba
Drum Alley, High Holbourn 3Ac
Drury Lane, St. Giles's in the Fields 11Ba 3Ac 3Bc
Dry Dock 16Ab
Duals Alley, High Holbourn 3Bc
Duchy Lane, Strand 11Ba
Duck Lane, Peter Street 18Ca
Duck Lane, West Smithfield 4Cc
Ducking Pond, Ducking Pond Row 7Ab
Ducking Pond Lane, Mile End, New Town 7Ab 7Ac
Ducking Pond Row, near Mile End New Town 7Ab 7Ac
Duet's Wharf, Lemon Street, and Milk Yard 14Ba
Duffins Alley, King Street, Westminster 11Ac
Duke of Norfolk's Yard, St. Albans Street 10Cb
Duke Shore Alley, Duke Shore 16Bb
Duke Shore Stairs, near Grave's Dock, Limehouse 16Bb
Duke Street, Artillery Lane 6Ac
Duke Street Chapel, Westminster 10Cc
Duke Street, Gravel Lane 12Cc
Duke Street, Great Germain Street 10Bb
Duke Street, Great Russel Street 3Ac
Duke Street, Lincoln's Inn Fields 3Bc 11Ba
Duke Street, Mint Street 13Ac
Duke Street, Tyburn Road 9Ca
Duke Street, Villiars Street, York Buildings 11Ab
Duke Street, Westminster 11Ac 10Cc
Duke's Court, Bow Street or Drury Lane 11Ba

Duke's Court, Great Almonry 18Ca
Duke's Court, Kingsland Road 6Aa
Duke's Court, Narrow Street, Limehouse 16Bb
Duke's Court, St. Martin's Lane 11Ab
Duke's Hospital, Pimlico 17Ca
Dun Horse Yard, St. Margaret's Hill 13Ac
Dung Wharf, Wapping Dock 15Ac
Dunghill Lane, High Timber Street 12Ca
Dunghill Mewse, near Hedge Lane 10Cb
Dunning's Alley, Bishopsgate Street 5Cc
Dunstan's Court, Fleet Street 12Aa
Dunster's Court, Mincing Lane 13Ca
Durham Court, Trinity Lane 13Aa
Durham Yard, in the Strand 11Bb
Dutch Churches:
 Austin Friars 5Bc
 at St. James's 10Bc
 in the Savoy 11Ba
Dutchy Lane, in the Strand 11Ba
Duxford Lane, Thames Street 13Ba 13Bb
Dye House, Booth Street 6Bc
Dye House, near Clink Yard, Clink Street 13Ab
Dye House, near the Narrow Wall 12Ab
Dye House, near St. Olave's Church, Tooley Street 13Bb
Dye House, Upper Ground 12Bb
Dyer's Buildings, Holbourn 4Ac
Dyer's Court, Aldermanbury 5Ac
Dyer's Court, Holbourn Hill 4Bc
Dyer's Court, Noble Street 4Cc
Dyer's Court Rents, near Skinners Hall, Dowgate Hill 13Aa
Dyer's Court Room, in Elbow Lane 13Aa
Dyer's Hall, Thames Street 13Bb
Dyers Yard, Church Lane, Whitechapel 6Bc
Dyot Street, St. Giles's Broad Street 3Ac

Eagle and Child Alley, Shoe Lane 4Bc
Eagle Court, St. John's Lane 4Bb
Eagle Court, in the Strand 11Ba
Eagle Street, Piccadilly 10Bb
Eagle Street, Red Lion Street 3Bb
Earl's Court, Great Earl Street 11Aa
East Harding Street, New Street 4Ac
East India House, Leadenhall Street 13Ca
East India Warehouse, Lime Street 13Ca
East Lane, Rotherhithe 22Ba 14Bc

East Lane Stairs, Rotherhithe 14Bc
East Rents, Griffis's Rent, Barnaby Street 13Cc
East Smithfield 14Bb
East Street, Red Lyon Street 3Bb
East Street, Spittlefields Market 6Ac
Ebbgate Lane, Thames Street 13Bb
Edlins Gate, Tooly Street 13Bb
Edmund's Court, Princes Street, Soho 10Ca
Edward Street Berwick Street 10Ba 10Ca
Edward Street, Hare Street 6Bb
Edward's Court, Oxendon Street 10Cb
Elbow Lane, Dowgate Hill 13Aa
Elbow Lane, near Gravel, Upper Shadwell 15Bb
Elder Street, White Lion Yard 6Ab
Elephant Lane, Rotherith 15Ac
Elephant Stairs, Elephant Lane, Rotherhithe 15Ac
Eliot's Court, Little Old Bailey 4Bc
Elizabeth's Court, Whitecross Street 5Ab
Elm Court, Elm Street 3Cb
Elm Court, Middle Temple 12Aa
Elm Row, Sun Tavern Fields 15Ca
Elm Street, Grays Inn Lane 3Cb
Ely Chapel, Ely House, Holbourn Hill 4Ac
Ely Court, Holbourn 4Ac
Embroiderers' Hall, Gutter Lane 4Cc
Emperor's Head Lane, Thames Street 13Aa 13Ab
Engine Street, Hide Park Road 9Cb
Entry, Kent Street 21Aa
Essex Court, Middle Temple 12Aa
Essex Court, Whitefriers 12Aa
Essex Road, beyond Mile End Old Town 8Ca 8Ba
Essex Stairs, Essex Street 12Aa 11Ca
Essex Street, in the Strand 11Ca
Euer Street, Gravel Lane 12Cc
Evangelists Court, Stone Cutters Alley, Black Friars 12Ba
Evans's Court, Basinghall Street 5Ac
Evans's Row, Old Bond Street 10Aa 10Ab
Exchange Alley, Cornhill 13Ba
Exchange Court, at Exeter Exchange 11Bb
Exchange Court, in the Strand 11Ba
Exchange, Rag Fair 14Bb
Exchequer, Westminster 19Aa
Excise Office, Old Jury 13Aa
Execution Dock Stairs, Wapping Dock 15Ac
Exeter Court, near Exeter Exchange in the Strand 11Ba

Exeter Exchange, Strand 11Ba
Exeter Street, Catharine Street 11Ba
Eyre Street, Leather Lane 4Ab

Fagers Alley, Turnmill Street 4Bb
Falcon Court, in the Borough 13Ac
Falcon Court, Fleet Street 12Aa
Falcon Court, Lothbury 13Ba
Falcon Court, near Rag Street, Clerkenwell 4Ab
Falcon Court, Shoe Lane 4Ac 4Bc
Falcon Court, Shoemaker Row, Aldgate 14Aa
Falcon Inn, Borough 13Ac
Falcon Lane, Falcon Stairs 12Bb
Falcon Stairs, Falcon Inn, Gravel Lane 12Bb
Falcon Yard, Kent Street 21Ba
Falconbridge Court, Hog Lane 2Cc
Falconers Alley, Cow Cross 4Bb
Fanns Alley, Goswell Street 4Cb
Farmer Street, Upper Shadwell 15Bb
Farmer's Alley, Hog Lane 2Cc
Farns Yard, Whitecross Street 5Ab
Farriers Yard, Stoney Lane 13Cc
Farthing Alley, East Smithfield 14Bb
Farthing Alley, Jacob Street, Mill Street 14Bc
Farthing Alley, in the Maze 13Bc
Farthing Pye House 2Ab
Farthing Street, Phenix Street 6Ab
Fashion Street, Brick Lane, Spittlefields 6Ac 6Bc
Feathers Court, Drury Lane 11Ba
Feathers Court, High Holbourn 3Cc
Feathers Court, Milk Street 13Aa
Featherstone Street, Brown Street 5Bb 5Ab
Featherston's Building, High Holbourn 3Cc
Fell Court, Fell Street, Wood Street 5Ac
Fell Street, Little Wood Street 5Ac
Fellmongers, Barnaby Street 13Cc
Fen Court, Fenchurch Street 13Ca
Fen Court, St. Michael's Lane 13Bb
Fenchurch Buildings, Fenchurch Street 13Ca
Fenchurch Street, Grace Church Street 13Ca
Fetter Lane, Fleet Street 4Ac 12Aa
Field Court, Gray's Inn 3Cc
Field Lane, Holbourn Hill 4Bc
Fig Tree Court, Barbican 4Cb 4Cc
Fig Tree Court, Middle Temple 12Aa

Finch Lane, Cornhill 13Ba
Finsbury Mewse, Chiswell Street 5Bb
Finsbury, Moorfields 5Bc 5Bb
Finsbury Yard, Chiswel Street 5Bb
Fire Ball Alley, Houndsditch 6Ac 5Cc
Fire Ball Court, Houndsditch 6Ac
Fire Office, Gutter Lane 4Cc
Fire Office, St. Martin's Lane 11Aa
First Postern, London Wall 5Ac
Fish Market, Bloomsbury 3Ac
Fish Market, Leadenhall 13Ca
Fish Street Hill, Grace Church Street 13Ba 13Bb
Fishers Alley, Petticoat Lane 6Ac
Fishers Alley, Water Lane, Fleet Street 12Ba 12Aa
Fishers Court, Eagle Street 3Cc
Fisher's Street, Red Lion Square 3Bc
Fishmonger's Alley, Fenchurch Street 13Ca
Fishmonger's Alley, St. Margaret's Hill 13Ac
Fishmonger's Alms Houses, Newington Butts 20Bb 20Cb 20Ac
Fishmongers' Hall, near the Old Swan 13Bb
Fitche's Court, Noble Street 5Ac 4Cc
Five Feet Lane, Thames Street 12Ca
Five Fields, Chelsea 17Cb 17Ca
Five Fields Row, Chelsea 17Bb
Five Foot Lane, Barnaby Street 13Cc 22Aa 14Ac
Five Inkhorn Court, Petticoat Lane 6Ac
Five Inkhorn Court, Whitechapel 6Bc
Flamton Court, Fore Street 5Bc
Fleet Bridge, Fleet Street 12Ba
Fleet Ditch, Fleet Bridge 12Ba
Fleet Lane, Old Bailey 4Bc
Fleet Market, Fleet Street 4Bc 12Ba
Fleet Prison, Fleet Market 12Ba 4Ac
Fleet Street, Fleet Bridge 12Aa 12Ba
Fleet Street, New George Street, Spittlefields 6Bb
Flemish Churchyard:
  St. Catharine's Lane 14Ab
  Tower Ditch 14Ab
Fletchers' Hall, St. Mary Axe 13Ca
Flower and Dean Street, Brick Lane, Spittlefields 6Ac 6Bc
Flower de Luce Alley, Wheeler Street 6Ab
Flower de Luce Court, Blackfriars 12Ba
Flower de Luce Court, Bristol Street, Puddle Dock 12Ba
Flower de Luce Court, Fleet Street 12Aa 4Ac

Flower de Luce Court, Gray's Inn Lane 3Cb
Flower de Luce Court, Tooly Street 13Bb 13Bc
Flower de Luce Court, Turnmill Street 4Bb
Flower de Luce Court, White Horse Alley, Cowcross 4Bb
Flower de Luce Street, Elder Street 6Ab
Flower de Luce Yard, Tooley Street 13Bc 13Bb
Flying Horse Court, Grub Street 5Ac
Flying Horse Yard, Bartholomew Close 4Cc
Flying Horse Yard, Bishopsgate Street 5Cc
Flying Horse Yard, Blackman Street 21Aa
Flying Horse Yard, Broad Street 5Bc
Flying Horse Yard, Fleet Street 12Aa
Flying Horse Yard, Half Moon Alley, Bishopsgate Street 5Cc
Folly, near St. Saviours Dock 14Bc
Foot Path to Bow 8Bb 8Cb
Fore Street, Lambeth 19Bb 19Bc
Fore Street, Limehouse 16Cb
Fore Street, near Moorgate 5Ac 5Bc
Fort Street, Spittle Square 6Ac 6Ab
Foster Lane, Cheapside 4Cc 12Ca
Fosters Buildings, Whitecross Street 5Ab
Fouberts Passage, Great Swallow Street 10Ba
Foul Lane, in the Borough 13Ab 13Bb
Founders Court, Fore Street 5Ac
Founders Court, Lothbury 13Ba
Founder's Hall, Founders Court, Lothbury 13Ba
Foundling Hospital, Lambs Conduit Fields 3Bb 3Ba
Fountain Alley, Maiden Lane, Gravel Lane 13Ab
Fountain Court, Aldermanbury 5Ac
Fountain Court, Cheapside 12Ca
Fountain Court, Middle Temple 12Aa
Fountain Court, in the Minories 14Aa
Fountain Court, in the Strand 11Ba
Fountain Stairs, Rotherhithe 14Cc
Four Dove Court, St. Martin's le Grand 4Cc
Four Swan Yard, Mile End Green 7Bc
Four Swans Inn, Bishopsgate Street 5Cc
Fox Court, Fox Lane, Wapping 15Bb
Fox Court, Grays Inn Lane 4Ac
Fox Court, Queen Square 3Bb
Fox Court, St. James's Street 10Bb
Fox and Crown Court, Barbican 4Cb
Fox and Goose Yard, London Wall 5Ac
Fox and Goose Yard, Star Street, Wapping 15Bb
Fox and Hounds Yard, Bishopsgate Street 5Cc

Fox and Knot Court, Cow Lane 4Bc
Fox Lane, Upper Shadwell 15Bb
Fox Ordinary Court, St. Nicholas Lane 13Ba
Foxes Court, Cow Lane 4Bc
Foxwell Court, Charter House Lane 4Bc
Frame Work Knitters' Hall, Red Cross Street 5Ac
Francis's Court, Bartlet's Street 4Bb
Francis's Yard, Brook Street 15Ca
Franklin's Row, Chelsea 17Ac
Free School, Charles Street, Old Gravel Lane 15Ab
Free School, near St. Saviour's Churchyard 13Ab 13Bb
Free School Street, Horselydown 14Ac
Freeman's Court, Cornhill 13Ba
Freeman's Lane, Horselydown 14Ac
French Alley, Dorset Street 6Ac
French Alley, Goswell Street 4Cb
French Alley, near Old Street Square 5Aa
French Alley, Quaker Street 6Ab
French Charity Alms Houses, Corbets Court 6Ab
French Church:
  Berwick Street 10Ba 10Ca
  Brick Lane, 6Bc
  Brown's Lane 6Ab
  Hog Lane 10Ca
  Marybone Gardens 1Cb
  Orange Street 10Cb
  Parliament Alley, Artillery Ground 6Ac
  St. James's 10Bc
  St. John Street 6Bb
  St. Martin's Lane 13Ba
  Soho 10Ca
  Spring Gardens, Charing Cross 10Cb
  Threadneedle Street 13Ba
French Court, Pig Street 13Ba
French Court, Wentworth Street 6Ac
French Hospital, French Alley 5Aa
French Ordinary Court, Crutched Friers 13Ca
Fresh Wharf, Thames Street 13Bb
Friday Street, Cheapside 12Ca 13Aa
Frier's Alley, Wood Street 5Ac
Frier's Court, Old Street 4Cb
Frier's Court, Red Maid Lane 14Cc 14Cb
Friers Lane, Thames Street 13Ab
Friers Street, Shoe Makers Row, Blackfriers 12Ba
Friery, in Pallmall 10Bb 10Bc

Frog Island, Nightingale Lane, Limehouse 16Bb
Fryingpan Alley, Berwick Street 10Ca
Fryingpan Alley, Borough 13Bb
Fryingpan Alley, Fore Street, Lambeth 19Bb
Fryingpan Alley, Great Swan Alley 4Cb
Fryingpan Alley, Petticoat Lane 6Ac
Fryingpan Alley, Redcross Street 5Ab
Fryingpan Alley, Tothill Street 18Ca
Fryingpan Alley, Turnmill Street 4Bb
Fryingpan Alley, Wood Street 5Ac
Fryingpan Stairs, Cinnamon Street, Wapping Dock 15Bc
Frys Alley, Spring Street 15Bb
Fry's Court, Tower Hill 14Aa
Fullers' Alms Houses, near Camel Row, Mile End 7Bb
Fullers' Alms Houses, Hoxton Road 5Ca
Fuller's Court, East Smithfield 14Bb
Fuller's Rents, near Golden Lane 4Cb 5Ab
Fuller's Rents, High Holbourn 3Cc
Fullers Street, Hare Street 6Bb
Furnivals Inn Court, Holbourn 4Ac
Furnivals Inn, Holbourn 4Ac

Gainsford Street, Horsley Down Lane 14Ac 14Bc
Galley Key, Thames Street 13Cb
Garden Court, Middle Temple 12Aa
Garden Court, Petticoat Lane 6Ac
Gardiners Lane, King Street, Westminster 11Ac
Gardiners Lane, Petty France 18Ba
Gardiners Lane, near Willow Street 12Cb
Gardiners Row, Chelsea 17Ac
Garland Court, Stepney 8Ac
Garlick Hill, Thames Street 13Aa
Garter Court, Barbican 5Ab
Garter Yard, Ratcliff Highway 15Ab
Gatehouse Prison, Westminster 19Aa
Gaunt's Key, Thames Street 13Bb
Geneva Row, Tiburn Road 9Ca
George Alley, in the Borough 13Ac
George Alley, George Street, York Buildings 11Ab
George Alley, Holles Street, Clare Market 11Ca
George Alley, Lombard Street 13Ba
George Alley, Saffron Hill 4Bc
George Alley, Shoe Lane 4Bc
George Alley, Stony Street 13Ab
George Alley, Thames Street 13Bb

George Court, Bennet's Hill 12Ca
George Court, Coleman Street 5Bc
George Court, East Smithfield 14Bb
George Court, Gravel Lane 5Cc
George Court, Princess Street 10Ca
George Court, St. John's Lane 4Bb
George Inn, Aldermanbury 5Ac
George Inn, Aldersgate Street 4Cc
George Inn, Borough 13Ac
George Inn, Coleman Street 5Ac
George Inn, Grub Street 5Ac
George Inn, High Holbourn 3Cc
George Inn, King Street, Westminster 11Ac
George Inn, Leather Lane 4Ab
George Inn, Smithfield 4Bc
George Inn, Snow Hill 4Bc
George Inn, Whitechapel 6Bc
George Lane, Botolph Lane 13Ba
George and Plow Yard, Broadway 18Ca
George Stairs, Deptford 24Cb
George Stairs, Shad Thames 14Ac
George Street, near the Broad Place, Spitlefields 6Bc
George Street, Foster Lane 4Cc
George Street, Little Chapel Street 18Ba
George Street, in the Mint 12Cc
George Street, Ratcliff Highway 15Aa 15Ab
George Street, Tiburn Road 9Ba
George Street, York Buildings 11Ab
George Yard, Bow Lane 13Aa
George Yard, Dorset Garden, Fleet Street 12Ba
George Yard, Duke Street, Grosvenor Square 9Ca
George Yard, Fore Street, Lambeth 19Bb
George Yard, Golden Lane 5Ab
George Yard, Hog Lane, St. Gile's Pound 10Ca 2Cc
George Yard, King Street, Westminster 11Ac
George Yard, Lombard Street 13Ba
George Yard, Long Acre 11Aa 11Ba
George Yard, Old Street 4Cb
George Yard, Red Cross Street, Southwark 13Ac
George Yard, Shoreditch 5Cb
George Yard, near Sturts Alley, Kent Street 21Aa
George Yard, Thames Street 12Ca
George Yard, Tower Hill 14Ab
George Yard, Turnmill Street 4Bb
George Yard, Whitechapel 6Bc

George's Buildings, Catherine Wheel Alley, White Chapel 6Bc
George's Court, Hatton Wall 4Ab
George's Court, Near Newington Turnpike 20Ca
German Church:
    at St. James's 10Bc
    in the Savoy 11Bb 11Ba
Gerrard Street, Prince's Street, Soho 10Ca
Gerrard's Hall Inn, Basing Lane 13Aa
Gibraltar, near Virginia Row, Shoreditch 6Ba
Gibson's Court, Marybone Street 10Bb
Gilbert Street, Bloomsbury 3Ac
Gilham's Court, Rotherhithe Wall 15Ac
Gilham's Rents, The Folly, Dock Head 14Bc
Gilly Key, Thames Street 13Cb
Giltspur Street, without Newgate 4Bc
Gingerbread Alley, Old Change 12Ca
Gingerbread Court, Lamb Alley, Bishopsgate Street 5Cc
Girdlers' Alms Houses, near Old Street 5Aa
Girdlers' Hall, Basinghall Street 5Ac
Glassenbury Court, Rose Street 11Aa
Glasshouse Alley, White Friers 12Aa
Glasshouse Fields, near Brook Street 15Ca
Glasshouse, Glass House Yard, Goodman's Fields 14Aa
Glasshouse Hill, Well Street 14Bb 14Ba
Glasshouse Street, Little Swallow Street 10Ba
Glasshouse Yard, Blackfriers 12Ba
Glasshouse Yard, Glasshouse Hill, Well Street 14Bb
Glasshouse Yard, Goodman's Yard, Goodman's Fields 14Aa
Glasshouse Yard, Green Walk, Upper Ground 12Bb
Glasshouse Yard, near Old Barge Stairs 12Ab
Glasshouse Yard, Pickax Street 4Cb
Glasshouse Yard, Red Maid Lane 14Cc
Glasshouse Yard, Whites Yard 14Bb
Glasshouse Yard, Willow Street 12Cb
Globe Alley, Deadman's Place 13Ab
Globe Alley, Fish Street Hill 13Bb
Globe Alley, Narrow Street, Limehouse 16Bb
Globe Alley, Wapping 14Cc
Globe Court, Shoe Lane 12Ba
Globe Island, near Wright Street, Rotherhith 16Ab
Globe Lane, Mile End 7Ca
Globe Stairs, Rotherhithe 16Ab
Globe Yard, Schoolhouse Lane, Ratcliff 15Ca
Gloucester Court, Beer Lane 13Cb
Gloucester Court, St. James's Street 10Bb

64

Hanging Sword Alley, Water Lane 12Aa
Hanging Sword Court, Fleet Street 12Aa
Hangman's Gains Alley, St. Catharine's 14Ab
Hangmans Gains, St. Cathinns 14Ab
Hanover Court, Grub Street 5Ac
Hanover Court, Houndsditch 14Aa
Hanover Square 10Aa
Hanover Stairs, Hanover Street 15Bc
Hanover Street, Hanover Square 10Aa
Hanover Street, Long Acre 11Aa
Hanover Street, Redriff Wall 15Bc
Hanway Street, Tottenham Court Road 2Cc
Harcourt Buildings, in the Temple 12Aa
Hare Alley, Shoreditch 6Aa
Hare Court, Aldersgate Street 4Cc
Hare Court, Frying Pan Alley, Petticoat Lane 6Ac
Hare Court, Inner Temple 12Aa
Hare Court, Upper Ground 12Bb
Hare Marsh, Hare Street 6Cb
Hare Street, Spittlefields 6Bb 6Cb
Harp Alley, Grub Street 5Ac
Harp Alley, Saffron Hill 4Bc
Harp Alley, Shoe Lane 4Bc
Harp Court, Little Knight Riders Street 12Ca
Harp Inn, Kent Street 21Ba
Harp Lane, Tower Street 13Cb
Harper's Walk, Fore Street, Lambeth 19Bb
Harris's Court, Brook Street 16Aa
Harris's Court, Ratcliff Highway 15Ab
Harrow Alley, near Mint Street 13Ac
Harrow Alley, Old Gravel Lane 15Ab
Harrow Alley, Petticoat Lane 6Ac
Harrow Alley, Whitechapel 14Aa
Harrow Corner, Deadman's Place 13Ab
Harrow Court, Bennet's Hill 12Ca
Harrow Dunghill, Mint Street 13Ac
Harrow Yard, Ropemakers Field 16Cb
Hart Row Street, without Newgate 4Bc
Hart Street, Bloomsbury Square 3Ac
Hart Street, Cripplegate 5Ac
Hart Street, Duke Street, Grosvenor Square 9Ca 9Ba
Hart Street, Mark Lane 13Ca
Hartshorn Court, Golden Lane, Old Street 5Ab
Hartshorn Lane, in the Strand 11Ab
Harwood's Court, Well Close Square and Well Street 14Bb

Hass Park, Wheeler Street 6Ab
Hasting's Court, Ratcliff Highway 15Aa
Hat and Mitre Court, St. John's Street 4Bb
Hatchet Alley, Church Lane, Whitechapel 6Bc
Hatchet Alley, East Smithfield 14Bb
Hatchet Alley, Little Tower Hill 14Ab
Hatfield Street, Goswell Street 4Cb
Hatton Court, Saffron Hill 4Bc
Hatton Court, Threadneedle Street 13Ba
Hatton Garden, Holbourn 4Ab 4Ac
Hatton Street, vulg. Hatton Garden 4Ac 4Ab
Hatton Wall, Hatton Garden 4Ab
Hatton Yard, Hatton Wall 4Ab
Haunch of Venison, Brook Street Yard 9Ca
Hawkin's Court, St. Michael's Lane 13Ba
Hay Court, King Street, near Newport Market 10Ca
Hay Hill, Dover Street 10Ab
Hay Market, near Charing Cross 10Cb
Hazlewood Court, Blue Anchor Alley, Bunhill Row 5Ab
Heathcock Court, in the Strand 11Bb
Heath's Rents, Church Lane, Rag Fair 14Ca 14Ba
Heddon Street, near Swallow Street 10Ba
Heddon's Court, Swallow Street 10Ba
Hedge Lane, Charing Cross 10Cb
Helmet Alley, Fore Street 5Ac
Helmet Court, Butcher Row 14Bb
Helmet Court, Fore Street 5Ac
Helmet Court, London Wall 5Ac
Helmet Court, in the Strand 11Ba
Helmet Court, Thames Street 12Ca
Helmet Court, Wormwood Street 5Cc
Helmet Row, Old Street 5Aa 5Ab
Hemlock Court, Carey Street 11Ca
Hemming's Row, St. Martin's Lane 11Ab
Hemp Yard, Seething Lane 13Ca
Hen and Chickens Court, Fleet Street 12Aa
Henage Lane, Duke's Place 13Ca
Henrietta Street, Cavendish Square 1Cc 2Ac
Henrietta Street, Covent Garden 11Aa 11Ba
Henry Street, Old Street 5Aa
Hepper's Wharf, Thames Street, near Puddle Dock 12Ba
Herald's College or Office, Bennet's Hill 12Ca
Herb Market, Leadenhall 13Ca
Hercules Pillars Alley, Fleet Street 12Aa
Hercules Yard, Turnmill Street 4Bb

Hermitage Bridge, Hermitage Dock 14Bb 14Bc
Hermitage Dock, Hermitage Bridge, St. Catherine's 14Bb 14Bc
Hermitage Stairs, Little Hermitage, Wapping 14Bc
Hewet's Court, in the Strand 11Ab
Hewey Court, near Halfmoon Street, Strand 11Ab
Heyden Yard, in the Minories 14Aa
Heydon Court, Heydon Square 14Aa
Heydon Passage, Heydon Square 14Aa
Heydon Square, Minories 14Aa
Hick's Court, Shoreditch 5Ca
Hicks's Hall, St. John Street 4Bb
Hide Park 9Ab
Hide Park Corner 9Cc
Hide Park Gate and Lodge 9Bc
Hide Street, Bloomsbury Market 3Ac
Hide's Rents, Chick Lane 4Bc
High Holbourn, near St. Giles's 3Bc 3Cc
High Street, Aldgate 14Aa
High Street, St. Giles's 2Cc
High Street, near White Chapel 6Bc 6Cc
High Timber Street, Broken Wharf, Thames Street 12Ca
Highgate Road, Tottenham Court 2Ba
Hill and Kifford's Alms Houses, Petty France, Westminster 18Ba
Hill, The, St. John's Street 6Bb
Hill's Alms Houses, near Artillery Ground, Westminster 18Ba 18Bb
Hill's Rents, Helmet Court, Butcher Row 14Bb
Hilliard's Court, Old Gravel Lane 15Ac 15Ab
Hind Court, Fleet Street 12Aa
Hind's Alley, Maiden Lane 12Cb
Hinton's Alms Houses, Plow Alley, Barbican 4Cb
Hoars Yard, Angel Alley, Bishopsgate Street 5Cc
Hockenhull's Court, Black Eagle Street 6Ab
Hockley Hole, Hockley in the Hole 4Ab
Hockley in the Hole Street 4Ab
Hog Alley, East Smithfield 14Bb
Hog Lane, Norton Falgate 5Cb 5Bb
Hog Lane, St. Giles's Pound 10Ca 2Cc
Hog Yard, Flemish Church Yard, St. Catherin's Alley 14Ab
Hog Yard, Liquor Pond Street 4Ab
Hog Yard, White's Yard, Rosemary Lane 14Ba 14Bb
Holand Street, Great Wardour Street 2Bc
Holand Street, Water Lane, Blackfriers 12Ba

Holbourn 3Cc 4Ac
Holbourn Bars, Holbourn 4Ac
Holbourn Bridge, Holbourn 4Bc
Holbourn Court, Gray's Inn 3Cc 4Ac
Holbourn Hill, Holbourn 4Ac 4Bc
Holbourn Row, Lincoln's Inn Fields 3Cc
Hole in the Wall, Little Russel Street 3Ac
Holford Court, Fenchurch Street 13Ca
Holiday's Court, Blue Anchor Alley 14Bb
Holland's Yard, Creed Lane 12Ba
Holland Street, Great Wardour Street 2Bc
Holland Street, Water Lane, Blackfriars 12Ba
Hollands Legar, near Green Walk 12Bb
Hollis Street, Clare Market 11Ca
Hollis Street, Oxford Street 2Ac
Hollow, The, near Brick Lane 4Ca
Holiwell Court, Holiwell Lane, Shoreditch 5Cb
Holywell Court, St. Catharine's Lane 14Ab 14Bb
Holywell Lane, Shoreditch 5Cb
Holywell Mount, Holywell Lane 5Cb
Holywell Street, in the Strand 11Ca
Honesty Square, St. John's Court, Chick Lane 4Bc
Honey Lane, Cheapside 13Aa
Honey Lane Market, Milk Street 13Aa
Honey Suckle Court, Grub Street 5Ac
Hooker's Court, St. Nicholas Lane 13Ba
Hoop Alley, Old Street 4Cb
Hoop Alley, Portpool Lane 4Ab
Hooper's Square, Rupert Street 14Ba
Hop Garden, St. Martin's Lane 11Aa
Hopkins Street, Broad Street 10Ba
Hopton's Alms Houses, Green Walk 12Bb
Horn Alley, Aldersgate Street 4Cc
Horn Alley, Tower Street 13Cb
Horn Court, Basing Lane 13Aa
Horn Court, Peter Street 18Ca
Horn Yard, Blackcell Alley, Petticoat Lane 6Ac
Horn Yard, Goodman's Yard 14Aa
Horn Yard, Kent Street 21Aa
Horn Yard, Stoney Lane 13Cc
Horns Dock 16Ab
Horn's Yard Alms Houses, Cloth Fair 4Cc
Horns Yard, Cloth Fair 4Cc
Horns Yard, Whitechapel 14Aa
Horse Ferry, Lambeth 19Bb

Horse Ferry Lane, Fore Street, Lambeth 19Bb
Horse Ferry, Millbank 19Ab
Horse and Groom Yard, Wood Street, Westminster 19Aa
Horse Guards 11Ab
Horse and Trumpet Yard, Poor Jewry Lane 14Aa
Horse Walk, Windmill Hill 5Bb
Horseferry Road, Tothill Fields 18Ba 18Ca 18Cb
Horsemonger Lane, near Blackman Street 20Ca
Horseshoe Alley, Bankside 13Ab
Horseshoe Alley, Bunhill Row 5Ab
Horseshoe Alley, Fashion Street 6Ac
Horseshoe Alley, Moorfields 5Bc
Horseshoe Alley, Petticoat Lane 6Ac
Horseshoe Alley Stairs, Bank Side 13Ab
Horseshoe Court, Bridge Yard, Tooly Street 13Bb
Horseshoe Court, Clement's Lane 11Ca
Horseshoe Court, Peter Street, Hicks's Hall 4Bb
Horseshoe Inn, Blackman Street 20Ca
Horseshoe Inn, Goswell Street 4Cb
Horseshoe Passage, Blowbladder Street 12Ca
Horseshoe Yard, Brook Street 10Aa
Horsley Down Fair Street, near Free School Street 14Ac 13Cc
Horsley Down Lane 14Ac
Horsley Down New Stairs, Shad Thames 14Bc
Horsley Down Old Stairs, Horsleydown Lane 14Ac
Horsley Down Square, Shad Thames 14Bc 14Ac
Horsley Down Street, St. Olaves Street 14Ac 13Cc
Horsley Down, Tooley Street 13Cc
Hosier Lane, West Smithfield 4Bc
Hospital Walk, Hoxton 5Ca
Hot Water Alley, Paris Garden Lane, Upper Ground 12Bb
Houghton Street, Clare Market 11Ca
Houndsditch, near Bishopsgate 6Cc 14Aa
House of Commons 19Aa
House of Lords 19Aa
Hovell, Hog Lane, Norton Falgate 5Cb
Howard Street, Norfolk Street 11Ca
Hoxton Market, Hoxton 5Ca
Hoxton Road, Hoxton 5Ca
Hoxton, near Shoreditch 5Ca
Hoxton Square, Hoxton 5Ca
Huberts Yard, Browns Lane 6Ab
Huggin Alley, Huggin Lane 13Aa
Huggin Alley, Woodstreet 5Ac
Huggin Lane, Thames Street 13Aa

Hugh's Court, Water Lane 12Ba
Hungerford Market, in the Strand 11Ab
Hungerford Stairs, Hungerford Market 11Ab
Hunt Street, Spicer Street 6Bb
Hunt's Court, Castle Street, St. Martin's Lane 11Aa
Hunt's Court, Hunt's Street 6Bb
Husband's Street, near Berwick Street 10Ba
Hutchinson's Wharf, Milford Lane 11Ca
Hyde Park 9Ab
Hyde Park Corner 9Cc
Hyde Park Gate and Lodge 9Bc
Hyde Park, Bloomsbury Market 3Ac

Idol Lane, Tower Street 13Ca
Independent Meeting in:
Berry Street, St. Mary Axe 13Ca
Bull Lane, Stepney 7Cc
Collier's Rents, White Street 13Ac
Crispin Street, Spittlefields 6Ac
Deadman's Place, Southwark 13Ab
Fetter Lane 4Ac
Haberdasher's Hall, Staining Lane 5AC
Hare Court, Aldersgate Street 4Cc
Horsleydown 14Ac
Jewin Street, near Aldersgate Street 4Cc
Lime Street, near Leadenhall Street 13Ca
Moor Fields, Finsbury 5Bc
New Broad Street, near Little Moorgate 5Bc
New Crown Court, Carey Street 11Ca
Old Artillery Ground, Spittlefields 6Ac
Old Gravel Lane, Wapping 15Ac
Petticoat Lane, near Whitechapel 6Ac
Ropemakers Alley, Little Moorfields 5Bc
St. Michael's Lane, near Cannon Street 13Ba
Three Cranes, near Thames Street 13Aa
Ingram Court, Fenchurch Street 13Ba
Inner Scotland Yard, near Whitehall 11Ab
Inner Temple Lane, Fleet Street 12Aa
Innholders' Hall, Little Elbow Lane 13Aa
Insurance Office, Cornhill 13Ba
Insurance Office, Serjeants Inn, Fleet Street 12Aa
Ipswich Arms Inn, Cullum Street 13Ca
Ireland Yard, Puddle Dock Hill 12Ba
Irish Court, Whitechapel 14Aa
Iron Gate Stairs, Iron Gate, Tower 14Ab

Iron Gate, Tower and St. Catherines 14Ab
Ironmonger Lane, Cheapside 13Aa
Ironmonger Row, Old Street 5Aa
Ironmongers' Hall, Fenchurch Street 13Ca
Islington Road, Goswell Street 4Ca
Islington Road, St. John's Street 4Ba
Ivy Bridge Stairs, near the Strand 11Bb
Ivy Bridge, in the Strand 11Bb
Ivy Lane, Newgate Street 12Ca 4Cc
Ivy Street, Dyot Street 3Ac

Jack an Apes Row, Cheapside 12Ca
Jackson's Court, Curriers Alley, Blackfriers 12Ba
Jackson's Court, Gravel Lane 4Bb
Jackson's Court, White Street 13Bc
Jacob's Alley, Turnmill Street 4Bb 4Bc
Jacob's Street, Mill Street, Redriff 14Bc
Jacob's Well Yard, Nightingale Lane 14Bb
Jamaica Street, School Lane, Rotherhith 15Bc
James Court, Berry Street 13Ca
James Court, James Street, Featherstone Street 5Bb
James Court, James Street, Theobald's Row 3Cb
James Rents, Hermitage Dock 14Bb
James Street, north of Bedford Row 3Cb
James Street, Brooks Street 9Ca
James Street, Covent Garden 11Aa 11Ba
James Stret, Featherstone Street 5Bb 5Ba
James Street, Golden Square 10Ba
James Street, Hare Street 6Bb
James Street, Hay Market 10Cb
James Street, Hoxton Market 5Ca
James Street, Petty France 18Ba 18Aa 10Ac
James's Rope Walk, near Virginia Street 14Cb 14Bb
Jane Shore's Alley, Shoreditch 6Ab
Jasper Street, Aldermanbury 5Ac
Jeffrey's Square, St. Mary Ax 13Ca
Jenkin's Court, Ropemakers Field 16Cb
Jermain Court, Jermain Street 10Cb
Jermyn Street 10Bb
Jerusalem Court, Grace Church Street 13Ba
Jerusalem Court, St. John's Street 4Bb
Jerusalem Court, Shad Thames 14Ac
Jerusalem Passage, Ailsbury Street 4Bb
Jesuit's Ground, Savoy 11Ba
Jewin Street, Aldersgate Street 4Cc 5Ac

Jews Harp Court, Angel Alley, Bishopsgate Street 5Cc 5Cb
Jews Harp House, St. Mary le Bone 1Ba
Jews Old and New Burying Ground 8Ab
Jews Row, Chelsea 17Bc
Jews' Synagogue in:
Bevis Mark, Duke's Place 13Ca
Magpye Alley, Fenchurch Street 13Ca
Shoemaker Row, near Aldgate 14Aa
Jockey Field Row, near Gray's Inn 3Cc
John's Court, Cat's Hole, Tower Ditch, near Iron Gate 14Ab
John's Court, East Smithfield 14Ab
John's Court, Hannoway Street 2Cc
John's Court, Nightingale Lane, 14Bb
John's Street, David's Street 9Ca
John's Street, Gainsford Street 14Ac
John's Street, Golden Square 10Ba
John's Street, Ratcliff Highway 14Cb
Johnson's Court, Charing Cross 11Ab
Johnson's Court, Fleet Street 12Aa
Johnson's Street, Old Gravel Lane 15Ab
Joiner's Alley, Thames Street 13Aa
Joiner's Court, Jacob Street, Mill Street 14Bc
Joiners' Hall, Thames Street 13Aa
Joiners Street, Tooly Street 13Bb

Kemp's Court, Berwick Street 10Ba
Kempton Court, Vine Street 19Aa
Kennington Lane, Newington
Butts 20Bb 20Bc 20Ac 19Cc
Kent Road 22Ac 22Bc
Kent Street, Southwark 21Ba 21Aa 13Ac
Kettle Yard, Red Cross Street 13Ac
Key Court, Little St. Thomas Apostle's 13Aa
Kidney Stairs, Narrow Street 16Bb
King David's Fort, near Blewgate Fields 15Ba
King David's Lane, Upper Shadwell 15Ba 15Bb
King Edward's Stairs, Wapping Dock 15Bc
King Edward's Street, Tudor Street 12Ba
King Edward's Street, Wapping Dock 15Ac
King Henry's Yard, Nightingale Lane 14Bb
King James's Stairs, Wapping 15Bb
King John's Court, Barnaby Street 21Ca
King John's Court, Holiwell Lane 5Cb
King John's Court, Limehouse Corner 16Cb
King John's Court, Stepney Green 8Ac

King and Queen Stairs, Rotherhithe 15Cb
King's Arms Alley, Willow Street 12Cb
King's Arms Court, Ludgate Hill 12Ba
King's Arms Inn, Barnaby Street 21Ca
King's Arms Inn, Holbourn Bridge 4Bc
King's Arms Inn, Leadenhall Street 13Ca
King's Arms Stairs, College Street 11Bc
King's Arms Yard, Coleman Street 5Bc 5Ac
King's Arms Yard, Marybone Street 10Ba
King's Arms Yard, White Cross Street 5Ac
King's Arms Yard, Whitechapel 6Cc
King's Bench Alley, in the Borough 13Ac
King's Bench Prison, Borough 13Ac
King's Bench Walk, Inner Temple 12Aa
King's Brewhouse, St. Catharine's 14Bb
King's Court, Nightingale Lane 14Bb
King's Gate Street, High Holbourn 3Bc
King's Head Alley, Broad Street, Radcliff 16Aa
King's Head Alley, Whitechapel 6Bc
King's Head Court, Beach Lane 5Ab
King's Head Court, Drury Lane 11Ba
King's Head Court, Fetter Lane and Holbourn 4Ac
King's Head Court, Fish Street Hill 13Bb
King's Head Court, Golden Lane 4Cb 5Ab
King's Head Court, Gravel Lane 5Cc
King's Head Court, Little Carter Lane 12Ca
King's Head Court, Petticoat Lane 6Ac
King's Head Court, St. Martin's le Grand 4Cc
King's Head Court, Shoe Lane 4Ac 4Bc
King's Head Court, Tenter Ground, Rose Lane 6Ac
King's Head Court, Whitecross Street 5Ac
King's Head Inn, Borough 13Ac 13Bc
King's Head Inn, Old Change 12Ca
King's Head Inn, Smithfield 4Bc
King's Head Yard, Fore Street, Lambeth 19Bb
King's Head Yard, High Holbourn 3Bc
King's Head Yard, Leather Lane 4Ab
King's Head Yard, Nightingale Yard 14Bb
King's Head Yard, Tooley Street 13Cc 13Bc
King's Mill, near Russel's Mill Stairs 15Cc
King's Old and New Roads to Kensington 9Ac 9Bc
King's Printing House, Printing House Yard,
Water Street 12Ba
King's Road, Barnaby Street 21Ca
King's Road to Chelsea 17Ab 17Bb 17Ba 17Ca

King's Row, Shad Thames 14Ac
King's Square Court, Dean Street 10Ca
King's Square, or Soho Square 2Cc
King's Stairs, King Street, Rotherhithe 15Ac
King's Street, Berry Street, Dukes Place 13Ca
King's Street, Brick Lane, Spittlefields 6Ab 6Bb
King's Street Chapel 10Ba
King's Street, Cheapside 13Aa
King's Street, Compton Street, Wood's Close 4Ba 4Ca 4Bb
King's Street, Covent Garden 11Aa
King's Street, Gravel Lane 15Ab 15Bb 15Ac
King's Street, near Grosvenor's Square 9Ba
King's Street, High Holbourn 3Bc
King's Street, Hoxton Square 5Ca
King's Street, Little Tower Hill 14Ab
King's Street, in the Mint 12Cc
King's Street, New Monmouth Street 11Aa
King's Street, Old Greek Street 10Ca
King's Street, Old Street Square 5Aa
King's Street, Oxford Street 10Aa 10Ba
King's Street, Prince's Street, Soho 10Ca
King's Street, Ratcliff Highway and Princes Square 14Cb
King's Street, Rotherhithe Wall 23Aa 15Ac
King's Street, St. Bartholomew's Hospital 4Cc
King's Street, St. James's Square 10Bb
King's Street, Tooly Street 13Bb
King's Street, Upper Moorfields 5Bb 5Cb
King's Street, Westminster 11Ac
King's Street, Wood's Close 4Ba
King's Way, Gray's Inn Lane 3Cb
King's Yard, White Cross Street 5Ab
Kingsland Road, Shoreditch 5Ca
Kirby's Court, Chick Lane 4Bc
Kirby's Court, Foul Lane 13Ab
Knaves Acre, Old Soho 10Ca
Knight's Bridge Chapel 9Ac
Knight's Bridge, Hyde Park 9Ac
Knight's Court, Green Walk 12Bb
Knock Fergus, near Cable Street 14Ca

Labour in Vain Hill, Thames Street 12Ca
Labour in Vain Street, Lower Shadwell 15Bb 15Cb
Labour in Vain Yard, Labour in Vain Hill, Thames Street 12Ca
Lad Lane, Wood Street 5Ac

Ladle Court, Cuthroat Lane, Upper Shadwell 15Ca 15Cb
Lad's Court, Moses Alley, Willow Street 12Cb
Lady Clarks Yard, Gravel Lane 12Bb
Lady Dacre's Alm's Houses, near Petty France, Westminster 18Ba
Lady Leek's Grove, Mile-end Turnpike 7Bc
Lady Leek's Walk, Mile End Green 7Bc
Lady's Alley, Great St. Ann's Lane 18Ca
Lamb Alley, Bishopsgate Street 5Cc
Lamb Alley, Blackman Street 21Aa 13Ac
Lamb Alley, Clerkenwell Green 4Bb
Lamb Alley, in the Old Change 12Ca
Lamb Alley, St. Giles's Broadway 3Ac
Lamb Alley, Sherbourn Lane 13Ba
Lamb Alley, Whitechapel 6Cc
Lamb Court, Abchurch Lane 13Ba
Lamb Inn, behind St. Clement's 11Ca
Lamb Street, Red Lion Street, Spittlefields 6Ab
Lambert Street, Ayliff Street, Goodman's Fields 14Ba
Lambeth Butts, Lambeth 19Bb
Lambeth Hill 12Ca
Lambeth Marsh, Lambeth 19Ca
Lambeth Palace 19Ba 19Bb
Lambeth Road, Newington 20Bb
Lambeth School, Back Lane, Lambeth 19Bb
Lambeth Stairs 19Bb
Lamb's Chapel Court, Monkwell Street 5Ac
Lamb's Chapel, Lamb's Chapel Court 5Ac
Lamb's Conduit Mewse, Millman Street 3Bb 3Cb
Lamb's Conduit Passage, Red Lion Street 3Ca 3Cb 3Bb
Lambs Conduit, Red Lyon Street 3Bb
Lancaster Court, New Bond Street 10Aa
Lancaster Court, in the Strand 11Ab
Lane's Court, Cold Bath Square 4Ab
Langley Street, Long Acre 11Aa
Lang's Court, St. Martin's Street 10Cb
Last Alley, Whitechapel 6Bc
Lauderdale House, Aldersgate 4Cc
Laughton's Rents, Cinnamon Street 15Ab
Laurence Lane, Cheapside 13Aa
Laurence Poultney Hill 13Ba
Laurence Poultney Lane, Canon Street 13Ba 13Bb
Lavender Street, near Cuckold's Point 16Bb 16Ac
Leadenhall Market, Leadenhall Street 13Ca
Leadenhall Street, Cornhill 13ca

Leather Lane, Holbourn 4Ab 4Ac
Leatherseller's Hall, Great St. Hellens 13Ca
Lee's Court, St. Catharine's Lane 14Bb 14Ab
Lee's Street, Red Lion Square 3Bc
Leg Alley, Long Acre 11Aa
Leg Alley, Shoreditch 5Cb
Leg Court, Peter Street 18Ca
Legget's Walk, near Bull Alley, Upper Ground 12Ab
Leicester Fields 10Ca 10Cb
Leicester Street, Leicester Fields 10Ca
Leicester Street, Liquorpond Street 4Ab 3Bb
Leicester Street, Warwick Street 10Ba
Lemon Street, Ayliff Street, Goodman's Fields 14Ba
Lemon Street, Lowmans Pond Row 12Cc
Leopard Alley, Saffron Hill 4Ab
Leopards Court, Baldwin's Gardens 4Ab
Lewis Yard, Safron Hill 4Bc
Life Guard Yard, Oxford Street 2Bc
Lillypot Lane, Noble Street 4Cc 5Ac
Lime Street, Fenchurch Street 13Ca
Lime Street Square, Lime Street 13Ca
Lime Tree Court, Narrow Wall 11Cb
Lime Yard, Bristol Street, Puddle Dock 12Ba
Limehouse Bridge 16Bb
Limehouse Causeway 16Cb
Limehouse Corner, Limehouse 16Cb
Limehouse Dock, Narrow Street, Limehouse 16Bb
Limehouse Hole 16Cb
Limehouse Hole Stairs, Limehouse Hole 16Cb
Limekiln Dock, Limehouse 16Cb
Limekiln Hill, Limehouse 16Cb
Limekiln Yard, near Limekiln Dock 16Cb
Lincolns Inn 3Cc
Lincoln's Inn Chapel, Lincoln's Inn Old Square 11Cc
Lincoln's Inn Fields Square 3Cc
Lincolns Inn Gate 3Cc
Lincoln's Inn Grange 3Cc
Lincoln's Inn New Square, Searles Street 3Cc
Lincoln's Inn Old Square, Chancery Lane 3Cc
Lincoln's Inn Passage, Lincoln's Inn, New Square 3Cc
Lincoln's Inn Walks 3Cc
Linton's Court, Milk Yard, New Gravel Lane 15Bb
Lion Street, High Holbourn 3Cb
Lion in the Wood Inn, Wilderness, Dorset Street 12Ba
Lion's Court, Goldsmiths Alley, Luteners Lane 3Bc

Lions Inn, Wych Street 11Ca
Liquorpond Street, Leather Lane 4Ab 3Cb
Lisle Street, Prince's Street, Soho 10Ca
Litchfield Street, Soho 11Aa 10Ca
Little Almnery, Westminster 18Ca
Little Argyle Street 10Aa
Little Arthur Street, Great Arthur Street 4Cb
Little Ashen Tree Court, Water Lane 12Aa
Little Bacon Street, Brick Lane 6Bb 6Ab
Little Bailey Street, Little Tower Hill 14Ab
Little Bandy Leg Walk, Queen Street 12Cc
Little Bear Key, Thames Street 13Cb
Little Bell Alley, Coleman Street 5Bc
Little Booth Street, Brick Lane 6Bc
Little Bridges Street, Bridges Street 11Ba
Little Britain, Aldersgate Street 4Cc
Little Brook Street, Hanover Square 10Aa
Little Bush Lane, Thames Street 13Aa
Little Cable Street, Cable Street and Well Close Square 14Ca
Little Carter Lane, Old Change 12Ca
Little Castle Street, Winsley Street 2Bc
Little Catharine Street, Catherine Street in the Strand 11Ba
Little Chandos Street, St. Martin's Lane 11Ab
Little Chapel Street, Great Wardour Street 10Ba 10Ca
Little Cheapside, Three Cranes 13Aa
Little Cock Alley, Redcross Street 5Ac
Little Dean's Court, Dean's Court, St. Martin's le Grand 4Cc
Little Dean's Yard, near the Cloister's, Westminster 19Aa
Little Dice Key, Thames Street 13Cb
Little Distaff Lane, Old Change 12Ca
Little Drury Lane, in the Strand 11Ca
Little Earl Street, Seven Dials 11Aa
Little East Cheap, Fish Street Hill 13Ba 13Ca
Little Elbow Lane, Ratcliff High Way 15Bb
Little Elbow Lane, Thames Street 13Aa
Little Essex Street, Essex Street 11Ca
Little Friday Street Friday Street 12Ca 13Aa
Little Friers Gate, Fleet Street 12Aa
Little George Street, near the Broad Place, Spitlefields 6Ac 6Bc
Little Germain Street, St. James Street 10Bb
Little Gray's Inn Lane 3Cb
Little Greenwich, Aldersgate Street 4Cc
Little Grosvenor Street in Grosvenor Street 9Ca
Little Gun Alley, Green Bank, Wapping 14Cc

Little Hart Street, James Street, Covent Garden 11Aa
Little Hermitage Street, Wapping 14Bb 14Bc
Little Hollis Street, Hanover Square 10Aa
Little Ivy Lane, Ivy Lane 12Ca
Little Jermyn Street, St. James Street 10Bb
Little King Street, King Street, St. James's 10Bb
Little Knight Rider Street, Old Fish Street 12Ca
Little Lamb Alley, Blackman Street 13Ac
Little Lombard Street, Three Crane Lane 13Aa
Little Love Lane, Wood Street 5Ac
Little Marlborough Street, Carnaby Street 10Ba
Little Match Walk, Upper Shadwell 15Ba
Little Maze Pond, Snows Fields 13Bc
Little Maze Pond Street, in the Maze 13Bc
Little Mewse, Royal Mewse, Charing Cross 11Ab
Little Minories, Tower Hill 14Aa
Little Mitchel Street, Old Street 5Aa 5Ab
Little Montague Court, Little Britain 4Cc
Little Montague Street, Bell Lane, Spittlefields 6Ac
Little Moorfields, Fore Street 5Cb
Little Moorgate, London Wall 5Bc
Little Newport Street, Newport Street 10Ca
Little Old Baily 4Bc
Little Pearl Street, Vine Street, Spittlefields 6Ab
Little Peter Street, Tufton Street 19Aa
Little Portland Street, Portland Street 2Ac 2Bc
Little Prescot Street, Goodman's Fields 14Aa
Little Princes Street, Little Queen Street 3Bc
Little Queen Street, Holbourn 3Bc
Little Queen Street, King Street, Rotherhith 15Ac
Little Queen Street, Queen Street, Wapping 15Ab
Little Rider Street, St. James's Street 10Bb
Little Russel Street, Bloomsbury 3Ac
Little St. Andrew's Street, Seven Dials 11Aa
Little St. Anne's Lane, Peter's Street 18Ca
Little St. Helens, Bishopsgate 5Cc
Little St. Thomas Apostle 13Aa
Little Sanctuary, Westminster 11Ac
Little Sheer Lane, Sheer Lane 11Ca
Little Smith Street, Smith Street 18Ca 19Aa
Little Spring Street, Spring Street, Middle Shadwell 15Bb
Little Suffolk Street, Hay Market 10Cb 10Ba
Little Swallow Street, Piccadilly 10Bb 10Ba
Little Swan Alley, Goswell Street 4Cb
Little Swan Alley, St. John's Street 4Bb

Little Swan Alley in the Three Colt Yard, London Wall 5Bc
Little Sword Bearers Alley, Chiswell Street 5Ab
Little Three Tun Alley, Castle Street 6Ac
Little Tower Hill, Minories 14Ab
Little Tower Street, Tower Street 13Ca
Little Trinity Lane, Thames Street 13Aa
Little Turn Stile, High Holbourn 3Bc
Little Vine Street, Vine Street 10Bb
Little Warner Street, Cold Bath Street 4Ab
Little White Lion Street, Seven Dials 11Aa
Little Wild Street, Great Wild Street 11Ba 3Bc
Little Winchester Street, London Wall 5Bc
Little Windmill Street, near Golden Square 10Ba
Little Wood Street, Cripplegate 5Ac
Little York Street, Cock Lane, Shoreditch 6Ab
Lloyd's Court, Hog Lane 10Ca 11Aa
Lloyd's Yard, Goats Head Alley, Skinners Street 5Cc
Lock Hospital, Kent Street 21Ba
Lock Hospital, Pimlico Road 9Cc
Lock's Yard, Blackman Street 20Ca
Lodise's Alley, Salt Petre Bank 14Ba
Lodises Court, Saltpetre Bank 14Ba
Lombard Court, Seven Dials 11Aa
Lombard Court, West Street, Soho 11Aa
Lombard Street, Gracechurch Street 13Ba
Lombard Street, in the Mint 12Cc
Lombard Street, Wells Street 6Bb 6Bc
Lombard Street, Whitefriers 12Aa
London Bridge 13Bb
London Court, White's Alley, Rosemary Lane 14Ba
London House Yard, St. Paul's Churchyard 12Ca
London Infirmary, Goodman's Fields 14Ba
London Prentice Yard, Minories 14Aa
London Spaw, Bridewell Walk 4Aa
London Street, Fenchurch Street 13Ca
London Street, Mill Street, Rotherhithe 14Bc
London Street, Rose Lane, Ratcliff 16Aa
London Wall 5Ac 5Bc
London Workhouse, Bishopsgate Street 5Cc
London Workhouse Chapel, Bishopsgate Street 5Cc
Long Acre Chapel 11Aa
Long Acre, Drury Lane 11Aa
Long Alley, Cable Street 14Ca
Long Alley, Moorfields 5Cb 5Cc 5Bc
Long Cellar Court, St. Catharine's 14Bb 14Bc

Long Lane, Aldersgate Street 4Cc
Long Lane, Barnaby Street 21Ba 21Ca 13Bc
Long Walk, Christ's Hospital 4Cc
Long Walk, King John's Court, Barnaby Street 21Ca
Longditch, Westminster 10Cc 18Ca
Long's Alley, Roper Lane 14Ac 13Cc
Long's Court, Jamaica Street 15Bc
Looker's Court, King Street, Oxford Street 10Ba
Lord Cobham's Turnpike, near Wood's Close 4Ba
Lord Mayor's Dog House, Royal Row 5Bb
Lord Mayor's Mansion House 13Aa 13Ba
Loriner's Hall, London Wall 5Ac
Lothbury, Cateaton Street 13Aa 13Ba
Love Court, Mutton Lane 4Ab
Love Court, Petticoat Lane 6Ac
Love Court, St. Olave's Street 13Cc
Love Lane, Old Gravel Lane 15Ab 15Ac
Love Lane, Rotherhithe Wall 23Aa 15Ac
Love Lane, St. Mary le Bone 1Ba 1Ca
Love Lane, Thames Street 13Bb 13Ba
Love Lane, Willow Street 12Cb
Love Lane, Wood Street 5Ac
Love Yard, Green Bank, near Morgan's Lane 13Cc
Lovels Yard, White Cross Street, Old Street 5Ab
Lovet's Court, Pater Noster Row 12Ca
Lower Gun Alley, Greenbank, Wapping 14Cc
Lower Shadwell, near Shadwell Dock 15Bb
Lower Well Alley, Greenbank, Wapping 15Ac
Lower Wet Dock, near Deptford 24Bc
Lowman's Pond Row, Southwark 12Cc
Lowman's Street, Gravel Lane 12Cc
Loyds Yard, Goat's Head Alley, Skinners Street 5Cc
Lucas Street, Rotherhithe 23Aa
Ludgate Hill, Fleet Bridge and Ludgate 12Ba
Ludgate, Ludgate Street 12Ba
Ludgate Prison 12Ba
Ludgate Street, Ludgate 12Ba 12Ca
Lumley's Court, in the Strand 11Ba
Lutenors Lane, Drury Lane 3Bc
Lutheran Church, in Trinity Lane 13Aa
Lyme Street, Fenchurch Street 13Ca
Lyons Inn, Wych Street 11Ca
Lyons Key, Thames Street 13Bb

Macclesfield Street, Garrard Street 10Ca

Mad House, Bethnal Green 7Ba
Mad House, near Wood's Close 4Ba
Maddox Street, Great George Street 10Aa
Maggot's Court, Piccadilly 10Bb
Magpye Alley, Aldersgate Street 4Cc
Magpye Alley, Fenchurch Street 13Ca
Magpye Alley, Fetter Lane 4Ac
Magpye Alley, Gray's Inn Lane 4Ac
Magpye Alley, Wheeler Street 6Ab
Maid Lane, Gravel Lane 12Cb 13Ab
Maiden Lane, Halfmoon Street 11Ba 11Aa
Maiden Lane, Queen Street 13Aa
Maiden Lane, Wood Street 4Cc 5Ac
Maidenhead Alley, Wapping 14Cc
Maidenhead Court, Aldersgate Street 4Cc
Maidenhead Court, Church Lane 6Bc
Maidenhead Court, Great Eastcheap 13Ba
Maidenhead Court, Great Gardens, St. Catharine's Lane 14Bb
Maidenhead Court, Grub Street 5Ac
Maidenhead Court, London Wall 5Bc
Maidenhead Court, Maiden Lane 13Aa
Maidenhead Court, Moor Lane 5Ac
Maidenhead Court, St. Thomas Apostles 13Aa
Maidenhead Court, Wheeler Street 6Ab
Maidenhead Inn, Great Knight Rider Street 12Ca
Maidenhead Passage, Berwick Street 10Ca
Maidenhead Yard, Dyot Street 3Ac
Mainard Street, Bembridge Street 2Cc
Malaga Court, Nightingale Lane 14Bb
Mallerd's Court, Blackboy Alley, Chick Lane 4Bc
Man in the Moon Yard, Chiswell Street 5Bb 5Bc
Manby Court, Montague Street 6Bc
Manchester Court, Channel Row, Westminster 11Ac
Manchester Stairs, Westminster 11Ac
Manoak's Alley, Shoreditch 6Ab
Mansel Street, Goodman's Fields 14Aa
Mansion House 13Aa 13Ba
Marble Hall, near Vaux Hall 19Ac
Margaret's Alley, Margaret Street 2Bc
Margaret's Street, Cavendish Square 2Ac 2Bc
Marigold Court, Barnaby Street 21Ca
Marigold Court, in the Strand 11Ba
Marigold Lane, Upper Ground 12Bb
Marigold Stairs, Marigold Lane, Upper Ground 12Bb
Marigold Street, Rotherhithe 22Ca 14Cc

Mariner's Alley, Fore Street, Lambeth 19Ba
Mark Lane, Tower Street 13Ca 13Cb
Market Court, Oxford Market 2Bc
Market Court, by Shepperds Market 9Cb
Market Hill, Upper Shadwell 15Bb
Market Lane, Pallmall 10Cb
Market Street, Germain Street 10Cb
Market Street, Oxford Market 2Bc
Market Street, Westminster 19Ab
Marlborough Court, Petticoat Lane 6Ac
Marlborough House, St. James's Park 10Bc
Marlborough (or Carnaby) Market, Carnaby Street 10Ba
Marlborough Mewse, Oxford Street 10Ba 2Bc
Marlborough Row, Carnaby Market 10Ba
Marsh Yard, Wapping 14Cc
Marshal Street, Carnaby Market 10Ba
Marshalsea Prison, Borough 13Ac
Marsham Street, Westminster 18Ca 19Aa 19Ab
Martin Court, Catharine Wheel Alley, Whitechapel 6Ac
Martin Street, Catherine Wheel Alley 6Ac
Martin's Court, Chick Lane 4Bc
Martin's Rents, Queen Street, King Street 15Ab
Martlet's Court, Bow Street 11Ba
Marybone Lane, Tyburn Road 1Cc
Marybone Passage, Oxford Street 2Bc 2Cc
Marybone Place, near Little Castle Street 2Bc
Marybone Street, near Warwick Street 10Ba
Mason's Alley, Basinghall Street 5Ac
Mason's Arms Yard, Madox Street 10Aa
Mason's Court, Brick Lane 6Bc
Mason's Hall, Basinghall Street 5Ac
Mason's Stairs, Bank Side 12Cb
Mason's Yard, North Audley Street 9Ba
Mast Yard, Wapping 15Bb
Match Walk, Upper Shadwell 15Ba
Matthases Court, Great Hermitage Street 14Cc
Maudlin's Rents, Nightingale Lane 14Bb
Maul's Court, Fore Street 5Ac
Maximus Court, Moorfields 5Bc
Mayfield's Buildings, Prince's Square 14Ca
Maypole Alley, in the Borough 13Ac
Maypole Alley, St. Olave's Street 13Cc
Maypole Alley, Wych Street 11Ca
May's Alley, Wheeler Street 6Ab
May's Buildings, Bedfordbury 11Aa

Mays Farm, Dog Row, Mile End 7Bb
Maze Court, Tooly Street 13Bc
Maze Pond, near Snows Fields 13Bc
Maze Pond Street, Southwark 13Bc
Maze Street, Tooly Street 13Bc
Mead's Court, Old Bond Street 10Ab
Meal Yard, Fleet Market 4Bc
Meard's Court, Wardour Street and Dean Street 10Ca
Mediford Court, Fenchurch Street 13Ca
Meetinghouse Alley, Green Bank 15Ac
Meetinghouse Court, Drury Lane 11Ba
Meetinghouse Court, St. Michael's Lane 13Ba
Meetinghouse Court, Stoney Lane 6Ac
Meetinghouse Ground, near Snow Fields 13Bc
Meetinghouse Yard, Devonshire Square 5Cc
Meetinghouse Yard, Five Foot Lane 14Ac
Meetinghouse Yard, near Gravel Lane 6Ac
Meetinghouse Yard, Maiden Lane, Deadman's Place 13Ab
Meetinghouse Yard, Nightingale Lane 14Bb
Meetinghouse Yard, Old Jewry 13Aa
Meetinghouse Yard, Water Lane 12Ba
Meetinghouse Yard, Wentworth Street 6Bc
Melancholy Walk, George's Fields 12Bc
Mercer Street, Long Acre 11Aa
Mercer's Alms Houses, Stepney Churchyard 8Ac
Mercers' Chapel, in Mercers' Hall, Cheapside 13Aa
Mercers' Court, St. Mary Hill 13Ca
Mercers' Court, Tower Street 13Ca 13Cb
Mercers' Hall, Cheapside 13Aa
Merchant Taylors' Alms Houses, Rosemary Lane 14Aa
Merchant Taylors' Hall, Threadneedle Street 13Ba
Merchant Taylors' School, Suffolk Lane, Thames Street 13Ba
Merchant's Water Works, Hartshorn Lane 11Ab
Merchant's Water Works, Rathbone Place 2Cc
Merlin's Cave, New River Head 4Aa
Mermaid Alley, Borough 13Ac
Mermaid Court 11Ab
Mermaid Court, Pater Noster Row, and Warwick Lane 12Ca
Mermaid Inn, Great Carter Lane 12Ca
Methodist Meeting in or near:
  Grey Eagle Street, Spitalfields 6Ab
  Nevil's Alley, Fetter Lane 4Ac
  St. Agnes le Clare 5Bb
  St. Martin's le Grand, near Aldersgate 4Cc
Snow's Fields, Southwark 13Bc

West Street, Seven Dials 11Aa
Windmill Hill, near Moorfields 5Bb
Mewse, near Millman Street 3Cb
Mewse, Devonshire Square 5Cc
Middle Moorfields 5Bb 5Bc
Middle Row, High Holbourn 4Ac
Middle Scotland Yard, Whitehall 11Ab
Middle Shadwell Lane, Virginia Planter Hill 15Bb 15Ac
Middle Shadwell, near Shadwell Market 15Bb
Middle Street, Cloth Fair 4Cc
Middle Temple Lane, Fleet Street 12Aa
Middlesex County Hospital, near Tottenham Court Road 2Cc
Middlesex Court, Drury Lane 11Ba
Middlesex Court, Little Bartholomew Close 4Cc
Middlesex Hospital, near Tottenham Court Road 2Cc
Milbourne's Alms Houses, Woodroff Lane 14Aa
Mile End Green, near Stepney 7Bb 7Cc 7Bc
Mile End Old Town 8Ab 8Bb
Milford Lane, in the Strand 11Ca
Milk Alley, Milk Yard, New Gravel Lane 15Bb
Milk Alley, near St. John's Church, Wapping 14Cc
Milk Street, Cheapside 5Ac 13Aa
Milk Yard, New Gravel Lane 15Bb
Milk Yard, Popping's Alley 4Bc
Mill Alley, Dean Street, Soho 10Ca
Mill Bank, Westminster 19Aa
Mill Lane, Tooly Street 13Cb 13Cc
Mill Pond Bridge, Rotherhithe 23Aa
Mill Street, Conduit Street 10Aa
Mill Street, Rotherhithe Wall 14Bc
Mill Yard, Rag Fair 14Ba
Miller's Court, Jasper Street 5Ac
Millman Street, near Red Lion Street 3Cb
Milkan's Wharf, Durham Yard, Strand 11Bb
Mincing Lane, Fenchurch Street 13Ca
Minories, Tower Hill 14Aa
Mint Square, Southwark 12Cc
Mint Street, near Mint Square, Southwark 12Cc
Mitchel Street, Brick Lane 4Ca
Mitchel's Court, Mitchel Street 4Ca
Mitre Court, Cheapside 12Ca
Mitre Court, Cornhill 13Ba
Mitre Court, Fenchurch Street 13Ca
Mitre Court, Fleet Street 12Aa
Mitre Court, High Street 14Aa

Mitre Court, Milk Street 13Aa
Mitre Court, St. Paul's Church Yard 12Ca
Moldstrand Dock Stairs, Willow Street 12Cb
Molin's Court, Shoe Lane 4Bc
Money Bag Alley, Blue Anchor Yard, Rosemary Lane 14Ba
Monkwell Street, Silver Street 5Ac
Monmouth Court, Hedge Lane 10Cb
Monmouth Court, Monmouth Street 11Aa
Monmouth Street, Black Eagle Street, Spitlefields 6Bb
Monmouth Street, near Seven Dials 11Aa
Montague Alley, Clare Street, Clare Market 11Ba 11Ca
Montague Close, in Southwark, 13Ab 13Bb
Montague Court, Bishopsgate Street 5Cb
Montague House, Duke of 3Ac
Montague Street, Brick Lane 6Bc
Montague Street, near Coxes Square 6Ac
Monument, Fish Street Hill 13Ab 13Ba
Monument Yard, Fish Street Hill 13Bb 13Ba
Moor Court, Fore Street 5Bc
Moor Lane, Fore Street 5Ac
Moorfields 5Bb
Moorgate, London Wall 5Bc
Moor's Alley, Nortonfalgate 5Cb
Moor's Street, Hog Lane, Soho 10Ca
Moor's Yard, Fashion Street 6Ac
Moor's Yard, Old Fish Street 12Ca
Moor's Yard, St. Martin's Lane, near the Church 11Ab
Morgans Ground, Chelsea 17Bc
Morgan's Lane, St. Olave's Street 13Cb 13Cc
Morris's Alley, New Lane, Shad Thames 14Bc
Morris's Causway Stairs 11Cb
Morse's Court, Nightingale Lane 14Bb
Mortimer Street, Cavendish Square 2Ac
Mortimers Yard, Woodroofe Street, Tower Hill 14Aa
Moses and Aaron Alley, Whitechapel 6Ac
Moses Alley, Willow Street, Bankside 12Cb
Moses Court, Moses Alley, Willow Street 12Cb
Mosley's Court, Philpot Lane 13Ca
Mould-maker Row, St. Martin's le Grand 4Cc
Mount Court, Gravel Lane, Houndsditch 6Ac
Mount Mill, Goswell Street 4Ca
Mount Pleasant, Great Warner Street 3Cb
Mount Pleasant, north of Little Greys Inn Lane 3Cb
Mount Row, David Street 9Ca
Mount Street, David Street 9Ca 9Bb 9Cb

Mouse Alley, East Smithfield 14Bb
Mudd's Court, Broad Street, Ratcliff 15Ca
Mulberry Gardens, Corporation Lane 4Bb 4Ba 4Ab
Mumford's Court, Milk Street 13Aa
Muscovy Court, Tower Hill 14Aa
Musickhouse Court, Shakespeare's Walk, Upper Shadwell 15Bb
Mutton Lane, Clerkenwell 4Ab
My Lady's Yard, Harrow Alley, Whitechapel 14Aa

Nag's Head Alley, Minories 14Aa
Nag's Head Alley, St. Margaret's Hill 13Ac
Nag's Head Court, Bartholomew Lane 13Ba
Nag's Head Court, Golden Lane 5Ab
Nag's Head Court, Gracechurch Street 13Ba
Nag's Head Court, Great Tower Hill 14Aa
Nag's Head Court, Snow Hill 4Bc
Nag's Head Court, Wentworth Street 6Bc
Nag's Head Inn, Whitechapel 6Bc
Nag's Head Yard, Great Swallow Street 10Aa
Nag's Head Yard, Norton Falgate 5Cb
Nailer's Yard, Silver Street, near Golden Square 10Ba
Naked Boy Alley, Barnaby Street 13Cc
Naked Boy Court, Little Elbow Lane 13Aa
Naked Boy Court, Ludgate Hill 12Ba
Naked Boy Court, in the Strand 11Ca
Naked Boy Yard, Back Lane, Lambeth 19Bb
Naked Boy Yard, Deadman's Place 13Ab
Narrow Street, Limehouse 16Ab 16Bb
Narrow Street, Ratcliff Cross 16Ab 16Bb
Narrow Wall, Lambeth 11Cb 11Cc 11Bc 12Aa 12Ab
Nassaw Street, Gerrard Street 10Ca
Navy Office, Crutched Friars 13Ca
Neal's Yard, Great St. Andrew Street 11Aa
Neat Houses, Chelsea Bridge 17Cc
Neckinger Road, Rotherhithe 22Ba
Nell's Wharf, St. Catharine's 14Bb
Nelson's Court, Drury Lane 11Ba
Neptune Street, Well Close Square 14Cb
Nettleton's Court, Aldersgate Street 4Cc
Nevil's Alley, Fetter Lane 4Ac
Nevil's Yard, Church Street, Lambeth 19Cb
New Bedford Court, Eagle Court, Strand 11Ba
New Belton Street, Brownlow Street 11Aa
New Bond Street, Oxford Street 10Aa

New Boswell Court, Carey Street 11Ca
New Broad Street, London Wall 5Bc
New Broad Street, near Moorfields 5Cc
New Buildings, Farthing Alley, Maze 13Bc 13Cc
New Buildings, Swan Alley, Coleman Street 5Bc
New Burlington Street, Swallow Street 10Aa
New Cock Lane, Brick Lane 6Ab
New Crane Stairs, Old Gravel Lane, Wapping Dock 15Bb
New Court, Blue Anchor Alley, Rosemary Lane 14Ba
New Court, Bow Lane 13Aa
New Court, Brown Street 5Ab
New Court, Carey Street 11Ca
New Court, Channel Row, Westminster 11Ac
New Court, George Yard, Whitechapel 6Bc
New Court, Goswell Street 4Cb
New Court, Great St. Anns Lane 18Ca
New Court, Harrow Alley, Petticoat Lane 6Ac
New Court, Hart Street, Crutched Friars 13Ca
New Court, Narrow Street, Ratcliff 16Aa
New Court, Newington Butts 20Bb
New Court, Nightingale Lane 14Bb
New Court, Pig Street 13Ba
New Court, Quaker Street 6Ab
New Court, St. Catharine's Court 14Ab
New Court, St. Swithin's Lane 13Ba
New Court, Throckmorton Street 13Ba
New Court, White Street 13Ac
New Exchange, Cable Street 14Ba
New Gaol, Borough 13Ac
New George Street, St. John's Street 6Bb
New Gravel Lane Alms Houses 15Bb
New Gravel Lane, Upper Shadwell 15Bb
New Inn, High Holbourn 3Cc
New Inn, Wych Street 11Ca
New Inn Yard, near Holy Lane, Shoreditch 5Cb
New Lane, Shad Thames 14Bc
New Nichol Street, Spittlefields 6Aa
New North Street, Theobald Row 3Bb 3Bc
New Palace Yard, Westminster 11Ac
New Paradise Street, Rotherhithe 23Aa
New Passage, Bull and Mouth Street 4Cc
New Passage, Newgate Market, to Ivy Lane 4Cc
New Peter Street, Peter Street 18Ca
New Prison, Clerkenwell 4Bb
New Prison Walk, Clerkenwell 4Bb

New Pump Court, Moor Lane 5Ac
New Pye Street, Pye Street, Westminster 18Ca
New Queen Street, Oxford Street 2Bc
New Rag Fair, East Smithfield 14Bb
New Rents, Compter Lane 13Ab
New Rents, St. Martin's le Grand 4Cc
New River Head and Water Works 4Aa
New Round Court, in the Strand 11Ab
New Square, Minories 14Aa
New Street, Broad Street 10Ba
New Street, Cloth Fair 4Cc
New Street, Dyot Street, St. Giles's 3Ac
New Street, Fore Street, Lambeth 19Bc
New Street Hill, New Street, Shoe Lane 4Ac 4Bc
New Street, Horselydown 14Ac
New Street, Lower Shadwell 15Cb
New Street, Old Street 5Aa
New Street, Queen Street, in the Mint 12Cc
New Street, St. Martin's Lane 11Aa
New Street, St. Thomas's Southwark 13Bc
New Street, Shadwell Market 15Bb
New Street, Shoe Lane 4Ac 4Bc
New Street, Shoemaker Row, Black Fryers 12Ba
New Street, Spring Gardens, Charing Cross 11Ab
New Street Square, New Street, Shoe Lane 4Ac
New Thames Street, Bank Side 12Cb
New Thames Street Stairs, Bankside 12Cb
New Tothill Street, Westminster 18Ca
New Tunbridge Wells, New River Head 4Aa
New Way, in the Maze, Tooley Street 13Bc
New Way, Orchard Street 18Ca
New Wells, Bridewell Walk 4Ab 4Cb
Newcastle Court, Butcher Row 11Ca
Newcastle Court, Newcastle Street, Chick Lane 4Bc
Newcastle Street, Chick Lane 4Bc
Newcastle Street, Seacoal Lane 4Bc
Newcastle Street, White Chapel 6Ac
Newel Street, Berwick Street 10Ba 2Bb
Newgate Market, Newgate Street 12Ca 4Cc
Newgate, Newgate Street 4Cc
Newgate Prison 4Bc
Newgate Street, Newgate 4Cc
Newington Butts 20Bb 20Cb
Newman's Court, Cornhill 13Ba
Newman's Court, Farmer Street 15Bb

Newmarket Street, Wapping Dock 15Ac
Newport Alley, Newport Street 11Aa
Newport Market, Newport Street 11Aa
Newport Street, Castle Street, near Newport Market 11Aa
Newton Street, High Holbourn 3Bc
Nichol Street, Spittlefields 6Aa
Nicholas Court, Rosemary Lane 14Ba
Nightingale Lane, East Smithfield 14Bb
Nightingale Lane, Limehouse 16Bb
Nixon's Court, Barnaby Street 13Cc
Nixon's Square, near Jewin Street 4Cc 5Ac
Noah's Ark Alley, Narrow Street, Ratcliff 16Ab 16Aa
Noble Street, Foster Lane 4Cc
Noble Street, Goswell Street 4Cb 4Ca
Noel Street, Burlington Gardens 10Aa
Norfolk Street, in the Strand 11Ca
Norris Street, in the Hay Market 10Cb
Norrison's Court, near Stangate 11Bc
North Audley Street, Grosvenor Square 9Ba
North Court, South Street 9Cb
North Passage, Well Close Square 14Ca
North Row, North Audley Street 9Ba
North Street, Spittlefields Market 6Ab 6Ac
North Street, Wood Street, Westminster 19Aa
Northumberland Alley, Fenchurch Street 14Aa 13Ca
Northumberland Court, Southampton Buildings, Chancery Lane 4Ac
Northumberland Court, Strand 11Ab
Northumberland House, Charing Cross 11Ab
Norton Falgate, Bishopsgate Street 5Cb
Norton Falgate, near Shoreditch 5Cb
Norwich Court, East Smithfield 14Bb
Nottingham Court, Castle Street, Seven Dials 11Aa
Nottingham Street, Plumb Tree Street 3Ac
Nuns Court, Coleman Street, 5Bc
Nutkins Corner, Rotherhithe Wall 14Bc

Oakey's Court, Hare Street 6Bb
Oakley's Yard, Tower Ditch 14Ab
Oat Lane, Noble Street 4Cc 5Ac
Oatmeal Yard, Barnaby Street 13Cc
Ocean Street, Stepney 8Ac
Off Alley, Villiers Street, York Buildings 11Ab
Ogle Street, Margaret Street 2Ac
Old Artillery Ground, Steward Street 6Ac

Old Barge House Stairs, near Glass House Yard 12Ab
Old Bear Garden, Maid Lane 12Cb
Old Belton Street, Short's Gardens 11Aa 3Ac
Old Bethlem, Bishopsgate Street 5Cc
Old Blue Boar Inn, High Holbourn 3Cc
Old Bond Street, Piccadilly 10Ab
Old Boswell Court, Clement's Lane 11Ca
Old Brewhouse Yard, Chick Lane 4Bc
Old Burlington Mewse 10Aa
Old Castle Street, Wentworth Street 6Ac
Old Change, Cheapside 12Ca
Old Exchange, Cable Street 14Ba
Old Fish Street Hill, Thames Street 12Ca
Old Fish Street, Little Knight Riders Street 12Ca
Old Gravel Lane, Radcliff Highway 15Ab 15Ac
Old Gravel Walk, Blue Anchor Alley, Bunhill Fields 5Ab
Old Jewry, Cheapside 13Aa
Old Nichol Street, Spittlefields 6Ab
Old North Street, Red Lion Square 3Bc
Old Packthread Ground, King's Road 21Ca
Old Palace Yard, Westminster 19Aa
Old Paradise Street, Rotherhithe 23Aa
Old Pav'd Street, Pall Mall 10Bb
Old Pipe Yard, Bristol Street, Puddle Dock 12Ba
Old Play House, Drury Lane 11Ba
Old Round Court, in the Strand 11Ab
Old Soho 10Ca
Old South Sea House, Broad Street 13Ba
Old Starch Yard, Old Gravel Lane 15Ab
Old Street, near Goswell Street 5Ab 5Aa 4Cb
Old Street Square, Old Street 5Aa
Old Swan Lane, Thames Street 13Bb
Old Swan Stairs, Ebbgate Lane 13Bb
Oliver's Alley, in the Strand 11Ba
Oliver's Court, Bowling Alley, Westminster 19Aa
One Mile Stone, Kent Street 21Ba
One Swan Yard, Bishopsgate Street 5Cc
One Tun Alley, Hungerford Market 11Ab
One Tun Yard, White Cross Street 5Ab
Onslow Street, Vine Street, Hatton Wall 4Ab
Opera House, Haymarket 10Cb
Orange Court, Castle Street 11Ab
Orange Court, Wapping 14Cc
Orange Street, Castle Street 10Cb 11Ab
Orange Street, Lowman's Street 12Cc

Orange Street, Red Lion Square 3Bc
Orange Street, Swallow Street 10Ba
Orchard, Butcher Row 16Aa
Orchard Street, Westminster 18Ca
Orchard, Wapping Dock 15Ac
Ormond Mewse, Great Ormond Street 3Bb
Ormond Yard, Great Ormond Street 3Bb
Oxendon Street, Coventry Street 10Cb
Oxford Arms Inn, Warwick Lane 12Ba
Oxford Arms Passage, Warwick Lane 12Ba
Oxford Chapel, Henrietta Street, Mary Bone 1Cc
Oxford Court, Oxford Street 10Aa
Oxford Court, Salter's Hall Court,
   St. Swithin's Lane 13Aa 13Ba
Oxford Market, Oxford Street 2Bc
Oxford Street, St. Giles's Pound 2Ac 2Bc 2Cc

Packers Court, Coleman Street 5Ac
Packson's Rents, Jamaica Street 15Bc
Packthread Ground, Bandy Leg Walk 12Cb
Packthread Ground, near the end of Barnaby Street 21Ca
Packthread Ground, near Maiden Lane 12Cb
Pageant's Stairs, Rotherhithe 16Bb
Page's Walk, King's Road 21Ca
Painter Stainer's Hall, in Little Trinity Lane 13Aa
Painters Court, Berry Street 10Bb
Painters Rents, Broad Street, Ratcliff Highway 16Aa
Pall Mall, St. James's 10Bb
Pallmall Court, Pallmall 10Cb
Palmer's Alms Houses, Horse Ferry Road, Chapel Street,
   Westminster 18Ba
Palsgrave Head Court, Strand 11Ca
Pancras Lane, Queen Street 13Aa
Pannier Alley, Newgate Street 12Ca
Panton Square, Coventry Street 10Ca
Panton Stables, Great Windmill Street 10Ca
Panton Street, Hay Market 10Cb
Paradise Court, Lady Clark's Yard 12Bb
Paradise Court, Peter Street 18Ca
Paradise Row, Brook's Street 9Ca
Paradise Row, Gravel Lane, near George's Fields 12Bc
Paradise Row, Lambeth 19Bb
Paradise Row, Tottenham Court Road 2Bb
Paris Garden Lane, Upper Ground 12Bb
Paris Garden Stairs, Paris Garden Lane, Upper Ground 12Bb

75

Plow Yard, Fetter Lane, Holbourn 4Ac
Plow Yard, Hartshorn Lane 11Ab
Plow Yard, Holbourn Hill 4Bc
Plow Yard, Seething Lane 13Cb
Plowman's Rents, Turnmill Street 4Bb
Plumb Tree Court, Plumb Tree Street 3Ac
Plumb Tree Court, Shoe Lane 4Bc
Plumb Tree Street, Broad St. Giles's 3Ac
Plumbers Court, High Holbourn 3Bc
Plumbers' Hall, Chequer Yard, Bush Lane 13Aa
Poland Street, Oxford Street 10Ba 2Bc
Poland Yard, Oxford Street 2Bc
Poor House, Denham Yard, Little Drury Lane 11Ba 11Ca
Poor Jewry Lane, Aldgate 14Aa
Pope's Head Alley, Broad Street 15Ca
Pope's Head Alley, Cornhill 13Ba
Pope's Head Court, Bell Yard 12Aa
Popping's Alley, Fleet Street 12Ba
Popping's Court, Popping's Alley 12Ba
Porter Street, Blossom Street 6Ab
Porters Block, Smithfield Barrs 4Bc
Porters Court, Basinghall Street 5Ac
Porters Field, Porters Street 6Ab
Porters Key, Thames Street 13Cb
Porters Street Alms Houses 6Ab
Porters Street, near Newport Market 11Aa
Portland Mewse 10Ba
Portland Street, Berwick Street 10Ba
Portland Street, Oxford Street 2Ac
Portpool Lane, Leather Lane 4Ab 3Cb
Portsmouth Corner, Lincolns Inn Fields 11Ca 3Cc
Portugal Chapel, Warwick Street 10Ba
Portugal Row, Lincoln's Inn Fields 3Cc
Portugal Street, Searle's Street,
  Lincoln's Inn Fields 3Cc 11Ca
Post Boy Passage, Shoemakers Row 12Ba
Post Office, Lombard Street 13Ba
Postern, Bakers Row 4Ab
Postern Row, Tower Hill 14Ab
Potage Pot Alley, Aldersgate Street 4Cc
Potters Fields, Pickle Herring Street 13Cc 14Ac
Poultry, near Cheapside 13Aa
Poultry Counter 13Aa
Pound, near Artillery Ground, Westminster 18Ba
Pound, St. John's Street 4Bb

Poverty Lane, Brook Street 9Ca
Powel's Alley, Chiswell Street 5Ab
Powel's Yard, St. Margaret's Hill 13Ac
Powis House, Ormond Street 3Bb
Presbyterian Meeting in or near:
  Broad Street, Wapping 15Ab
  Crosby Square, Bishopsgate Street 13Ca
  Crown Court, Russel Street 11Ba
  Founder's Hall, Lothbury 13Ba
  Grafton Street, Seven Dials 10Ca
  Gravel Lane, near Houndsditch 6Ac
  Hanover Street, Long Acre 11Aa
  King John's Court, Bermondsey 21Ca
  Leather Lane, Holbourn 4Ab
  Little Carter Lane, near the Old Change 12Ca
  Little Eastcheap, near Tower Street 13Aa
  Little St. Hellens, Bishopsgate Street 13Ca 5Cc
  Little Swallow Street 10Ba
  Long Ditch, Westminster 10Cc
  Maid Lane, near Deadman's Place 13Ab
  Meetinghouse Yard, Old Jewry 13Aa
  Middlesex Court, Little Bartholomew Close 4Cc
  New Broad Street, near Old Bethlem 5Cc
  Nightingale Lane 14Bb
  Parish Street, Horsleydown 13Cc
  Poor Jewry Lane, near Aldgate 14Aa
  Queen Street near Cuckold's Point 16Bc
  Ryder's Court, near Leicester Fields 10Ca
  St. Thomas Apostle, near Queen Street 13Aa
  St. Thomas Southwark 13Bc
  Salisbury Street, Rotherhithe 22Ca
  Salter's Hall, Cannon Street 13Ba
  Shakespeare's Walk, Upper Shadwell 15Bb
  Silver Street, near Wood Street 5Ac
  Windsor Court, Monkwell Street 5Ac
Prescot Street, Goodman's Fields 14Ba 14Aa
Price's Alley, Knaves Acre 10Ba 10Ca
Price's Court, Gravel Lane 12Bb 12Cb
Price's Yard, Long Lane 13Bc
Prichard's Alley, Horsleydown, Fair Street 14Ac
Priests Alley, Tower Street 13Cb
Primrose Alley, St. Mary Overies Dock 13Ab
Primrose Street, Bishopsgate Street 5Cb
Prince's Court, Drury Lane 11Ba
Prince's Court, Duke Street, Piccadilly 10Bb

Prince's Court, Hedge Lane 10Cb
Prince's Court, Long Ditch, Westminster 10Cc
Prince's Court, Lothbury 13Ba
Prince's Court, Old Gravel Lane 15Ab
Prince's Court, Wentworth Street 6Bc
Prince's Square, Ratcliff Highway 14Cb 14Ca
Prince's Stairs, Rotherhithe 15Ac
Prince's Street, near Back Lane, Sun Tavern Fields 15Ba
Prince's Street, Barbican 4Cb
Prince's Street, Brick Lane, Spital Fields 6Ac 6Bc
Prince's Street, Charles Street, Old Gravel Lane 15Ab
Prince's Street, Drury Lane 11Ba
Prince's Street, Duke Street 12Cc
Prince's Street, Hanover Square 10Aa
Prince's Street, Oxford Street 2Ac
Prince's Street, Red Lion Square 3Cc 3Bc
Prince's Street, Rotherhithe Wall 23Ba 15Ac
Prince's Street, Threadneedle Street 13Ba
Prince's Street, Upper Moorfields 5Bb 5Cb
Prince's Street, Whitcomb Street 10Ca
Printing House Street, Water Lane 12Ba
Printinghouse Yard, Printinghouse Street, Water Lane 12Ba
Privy Garden Stairs, Privy Garden 11Ac
Privy Garden, Whitehall 11Ac
Providence Court, North Audley Street 9Ba
Prujean Court, in the Old Bailey 12Ba
Pruson's Island, King Street, New Gravel Lane 15Bb 15Ab
Pudding Lane, Thames Street 13Bb 13Ba
Puddle Dock Hill, Great Carter Lane 12Ba
Puddle Dock Stairs, by Puddle Dock 12Ba
Puddle Dock, Thames Street 12Ba
Pulteney Court, Little Windmill Street 10Ba
Pulteney Street, Brewers Street 10Ba
Pump Alley, in Brown Street 5Ab
Pump Alley, Perkin's Rents 18Ca
Pump Alley, Queen Street, Park 12Cc
Pump Alley, Red Lion Street, Wapping Dock 15Ac
Pump Court, Bridgwater Gardens 4Cb
Pump Court, Inner Temple 12Aa
Pump Court, Jacob Street, Mill Street 14Bc
Pump Court, Minories 14Aa
Pump Court, Queen Hith 13Aa
Pump Court, White Hart Yard 11Ba
Pump Yard, Church Lane 16Cb
Pump Yard, Glasshouse Yard, near Aldersgate Bars 4Cb

Pump Yard, Golden Lane 4Cb
Pump Yard, Gravel Lane 5Cc
Pump Yard, King John's Court, Barnaby Street 21Ca
Pump Yard, Newington Buts 20Cb
Pump Yard, near Radcliff Cross 16Aa
Pump Yard, West's Gardens, New Gravel Lane 15Ab
Pump Yard, White Horse Alley, Cow Cross 4Bb
Punch Bowl Alley, Moorfields Quarters 5Bc
Purse Court, near Grub Street, Fore Street 5Ac
Purse Court, near Moor Lane, Fore Street 5Ac
Purse Court, Old Change 12Ca
Pye Corner, West Smithfield 4Bc
Pye Garden, near Willow Street 12Cb
Pye Street, Westminster 18Ca

Quakers Burying Ground 5Ab 21Ca
Quakers' Meeting in:
Devonshire Street, by Bishopsgate 5Cc
Ewers Street, Park 12Cc
Horsleydown, Fair Street 13Cc
Little Almonry, Westminster 18Ca
St. John's Street, the Peel 4Bb
Savoy in the Strand 11Ba
Schoolhouse Lane, near Brook Street 15Ca
White Hart Yard, Gracechurch Street 13Ba
Quakers Street, Brick Lane 6Ab 6Bb
Quakers' Workhouse 4Ab 4Bb
Queen Hithe Dock, Queen Hithe 13Aa
Queen Hithe Little Stairs, Queen Hithe 12Ca
Queen Hithe Stairs, Queen Hithe 13Ab 13Aa
Queen Hithe, Thames Street 13Aa
Queen Square Chapel, Westminster 10Cc
Queen Square, Little Bartholomew Close 4Cc
Queen Square, Ormond Street 3Bb
Queen Square, Westminster, near St. James's Park 10Cc
Queen Stairs, near Ratcliff Cross 16Ab
Queen Street, Bloomsbury 3Ac
Queen Street Chapel, Great Queen Street 3Bc
Queen Street, Cheapside 13Aa
Queen Street, Great Russel Street 3Ac
Queen Street, Great Windmill Street 10Ba 10Ca
Queen Street, Hoxton Market 5Ca
Queen Street, King Street, New Gravel Lane 15Ab
Queen Street, London Street, Ratcliff 16Aa 16Ba
Queen Street, Long Ditch, Westminster 10Cc

Queen Street Mewse, Great Queen Street 3Bc
Queen Street, in the Mint 12Cc
Queen Street, Old Paradise Street, Rotherhithe 23Aa 15Ac
Queen Street, Red Cross Street 12Cc 13Ac
Queen Street, Rosemary Lane 14Ab
Queen Street, Rotherhithe 16Bc
Queen Street, Seven Dials 11Aa
Queen Street, Thrift Street, Soho Square 10Ca
Queen Street, Tyburn Road 9Ca 9Ba
Queen's Arms Alley, Shoe Lane 4Bc
Queen's Arms Court, Upper Ground 12Bb
Queen's Court, Great Queen's Street 3Bc
Queen's Court, High Holbourn 3Bc
Queen's Court, King Street, Covent Garden 11Aa
Queen's Court, St. Catharine's Court 14Ab
Queen's Head Alley, Newgate Street 12Ca
Queen's Head Alley, Wapping Dock 15Ac
Queen's Head Court, Giltspur Street 4Bc
Queen's Head Court, Great Windmill Street 10Ca
Queen's Head Court, Turn-again Lane 4Bc
Queen's Head Inn, Grays Inn Lane 4Ab
Queen's Head Inn, St. Margaret's Hill 13Ac

Racket Court, Fleet Street 12Ba
Rag Fair, East Smithfield 14Bb
Rag Street, Hockley in the Hole 4Ab
Ragged Row, Goswell Street 4Cb
Ragged Staff Court, Drury Lane 3Ac
Raindeer Court, in the Strand 11Ba
Ralph's Key, Thames Street 13Cb
Ram Alley, Fleet Street 12Aa
Ram Alley, Fleet Street, near Spital Fields 6Bb
Ram Alley, near King and Queen Stairs, Rotherhithe 15Cb
Ram Alley, Wright Street, Rotherhith 16Ab
Ram Inn, Smithfield 4Bc
Ram's Head Court, Moor Lane 5Ac
Ranelagh Gardens, Chelsea 17Bc
Rat Alley, Great Eastcheap 13Ba
Ratcliff Cross, Ratcliff, near the Narrow Street 16Aa
Ratcliff Highway, near Upper Shadwell 14Cb 15Ab
Ratcliff Row, near Old Street 5Aa
Ratcliff Square, Ratcliff 16Aa
Ratcliff Street, Ratcliff High Way 15Ab
Ratcliffs Layer, Goswell Street 4Ca
Rathbone Place, Oxford Street 2Cc

Rebeccas Yard, East Smithfield 14Bb
Reckman's Rents, near Limehouse Bridge 16Bb
Red Bull Alley, St. Olave's Street 13Cc
Red Bull Alley, Thames Street 13Bb
Red Bull Court, Fore Street 5Ac
Red Bull Yard, Ailsbury Street, Clerkenwell 4Bb
Red Cow Alley, Church Lane, Rag Fair 14Ca
Red Cow Alley, Old Street 4Cb
Red Cow Inn, Whitechapel 14Ba
Red Cow Lane, near Mile End Turnpike 7Bb
Red Cross Alley, Borough 13Ac
Red Cross Alley, near Church Yard Alley Hole,
   London Bridge 13Bb
Red Cross Court, in the Great Old Bailey 4Bc
Red Cross Court, in the Minories 14Aa
Red Cross Court, Tower Street 13Cb
Red Cross Square, Jewen Street 4Cc
Red Cross Street, near Cripplegate 5Ab 5Ac
Red Cross Street, Nightingale Lane, and Butcher Row 14Bb
Red Cross Street, Queen Street 13Ac
Red Gate Court, in the Minories 14Aa
Red Hart Court, Fore Street 5Ac
Red Hart Inn, Fetter Lane 4Ac
Red Horse Inn, Old Bond Street 10Ab
Red Lion Alley, Barnaby Street 13Cc
Red Lion Alley, Cow Cross 4Bc
Red Lion Alley, Minories 14Aa
Red Lion Alley, St. John's Street 4Bb
Red Lion Back Court, Charterhouse Lane 4Cb
Red Lion Court, Charterhouse Lane 4Cb
Red Lion Court, Cock Lane 4Bc
Red Lion Court, Drury Lane 11Ba
Red Lion Court, Fleet Street 12Aa 4Ac
Red Lion Court, Grub Street 5Ab
Red Lion Court, Holbourn 3Cc
Red Lion Court, Holywell Lane 5Cb
Red Lion Court, Kingsland Road 5Ca
Red Lion Court, London Wall 5Bc
Red Lion Court, Long Acre 11Aa
Red Lion Court, Red Lion Street 6Ac
Red Lion Court, St. Catharin's Lane 14Ab
Red Lion Court, Silver Street 5Ac
Red Lion Court, Watling Street 13Aa
Red Lion Court, Wheeler Street 6Ab
Red Lion Court, White Hart Yard 11Ba

Sachell's Rents, near Church Street, Shoreditch 6Ba
Sacville Street, Piccadilly 10Bb
Sadler's Alley, Dorset Street 6Ac
Sadlers Arms Yard, Little Swallow Street 10Ba
Sadler's Court, Milford Lane, Strand 11Ca
Sadler's Hall, Cheapside 12Ca
Safron Hill, Field Lane, and Hockley in the Hole 4Ab 4Bc
St. Agnes le Clare, near Hoxton 5Ba
St. Alban's Church, Wood Street 5Ac
St. Alban's Street, Pallmall 10Cb
St. Alphage Church, near Sion College, London Wall 5Ac
St. Andrew Holborn Church 4Ac 4Bc
St. Andrew Holborn Churchyard, Eagle and Child Alley, Fleet Market 4Bc
St. Andrew Undershaft Church, St. Mary Axe 13Ca
St. Andrew Wardrobe Church, by Puddle Dock Hill 12Ba
St. Andrew's Court, Holbourn Hill 4Ac
St. Andrew's School, Hatton Garden 4Ab
St. Anne's Alley, Noble Street 4Cc
St. Anne's Church, near Aldersgate 4Cc
St. Anne's Church, Limehouse 16Ca
St. Anne's Church, Westminster, Dean Street, Soho 10Ca
St. Anne's Court, Dean Street 10Ca
St. Anne's Lane, Aldersgate 4Cc
St. Anthony, vulgarly St. Antholin's Church, Syths Lane, Watling Street 13Aa
St. Augustin, vulgarly St. Austin, Old Change, Watling Street 12Ca
St. Bartholomew the Great Church, West Smithfield 4Cc
St. Bartholomew the Less, in the Cloisters, West Smithfield 4Bc 4Cc
St. Bartholomew, near the Royal Exchange 13Ba
St. Bartholomew's Hospital, Smithfield 4Cc
St. Benedict, vulgarly Bennet Fink, Threadneedle Street 13Ba
St. Bennet's Church, Gracechurch Street 13Ba
St. Bennet's Church, Paul's Wharf 12Ca
St. Bennet Sherehog Churchyard, Pancrass Lane 13Aa
St. Botolph's Billingsgate Churchyard, Botolph Lane 13Bb
St. Botolph's Church, near Aldersgate 4Cc
St. Botolph's Church, near Aldgate 14Aa
St. Botolph's Church, without Bishopsgate 5Cc
St. Bride's Alley, St. Bride's Church 12Ba
St. Bride's Churchyard, Fleet Market 4Bc
St. Bridget, vulgarly St. Bride's Church, Fleet Street 12Ba
St. Catharine Coleman Church, in Fenchurch Street 13Ca

St. Catharine Creechurch, in Leadenhall Street 13Ca
St. Catharine's Church, St. Catharine's near the Tower 14Ab 14Bb
St. Catharine's Court, St. Catharin's 14Ab
St. Catharine's Lane, East Smithfield 14Ab
St. Catharine's Stairs, St. Catharine's 14Ab
St. Catharine's near the Tower 14Cc 14Bb
St. Christopher's Church, in Threadneedle Street 13Ba
St. Clement's Church, Clement's Lane, near Great Eastcheap 13Ba
St. Clement's Churchyard Strand, Alm's Houses 11Ca
St. Clement's Danes Church, in the Strand 11Ca
St. Clement's Danes Churchyard, Portugal Street 11Ca
St. Clement's Lane, Clement's Inn 11Ca
St. Clement's Lane, Lombard Street 13Ba
St. Dionis Backchurch, in Fenchurch Street 13Ba 13Ca
St. Dunstan's Alley, St. Dunstan's Hill 13Cb
St. Dunstan's Church, at Stepney 8Ac
St. Dunstan's in the East Church, St. Dunstan's Hill 13Cb
St. Dunstan's Hill, Thames Street 13Cb
St. Dunstan's in the West Church, in Fleet Street 12Aa
St. Dunstan's in the West Churchyard, Fetter Lane 4Ac
St. Edmond the King's Church, in Lombard Street 13Ba
St. Ethelberg's Church, in Bishopsgate Street 5Cc
St. Gabriel's Churchyard, Fen Court, Fenchurch Street 13Ca
St. George's Church, near Blackman Street 13Ac
St. George's Church, Botolph Lane 13Ba
St. George's Church, Hanover Square, in Great George Street 10Aa
St. George's Church, in Hart Street, Bloomsbury 3Ac
St. George's Church, in Queen Square 3Bb
St. George's Church, near Ratcliff Highway 15Ab
St. George's Fields, Southwark 20Bc
St. George's Hospital, near Old Gravel Lane 15Ab
St. George's School, Noel Street 10Aa
St. Gile's Church, by Cripplegate 5Ac
St. Gile's Church in the Fields, in St. Martin's Lane 3Ac
St. Giles's Court, St. Giles's Broadstreet 3Ac
St. Giles's, near High Holbourn 3Bc
St. Hellen's Church, in Great St. Hellens, by Bishopsgate Street 13Ca
St. James's Church, at Clerkenwell 4Bb
St. James's Church, in Duke's Place, near Aldgate 14Aa
St. James's Church on Garlick Hill 13Aa
St. James's Market, near the Hay Market 10Cb

St. James's Palace, St. James's Park 10Bc
St. James's Park 10Cc 10Bc 10Ac 10Cb
St. James's Place, St. James's Street 10Bb 10Ab
St. James's Square, Pallmall 10Bb 10Bb
St. James's Street, Pallmall 10Bb
St. James's Westminster Church, Piccadilly 10Bb
St. John Baptist Churchyard, Dowgate 13Aa
St. John the Evangelist's Burying Ground, Market Street 19Ab
St. John the Evangelist's Church, near Mill Bank 19Aa
St. John the Evangelist's Church Yard, Watling Street 12Ca
St. John Zachary's Churchyard, Maiden Lane 4Cc
St. John's Alley, St. Martin's le Grand 4Cc
St. John's Chapel, Chapel Street 3Cb
St. John's Church, at Clerkenwell 4Bb
St. John's Church, near Horsleydown 13Cc
St. John's Church, in the Savoy 11Ba
St. John's Church, Wapping 14Cc
St. John's Court, Cow Lane 4Bc
St. John's Court, Great Hart Street 11Ba
St. John's Court, St. John's Square 4Bb
St. John's Court, Somerset Street, White Chapel 14Aa
St. John's Gate, St. John's Lane 4Bb
St. John's Lane, St. John's Street 4Bb
St. John's Passage, St. John's Court 4Bb
St. John's Square, Clerkenwell 4Bb
St. John's Street, Islington Road 4Bb 4Ba
St. John's Street, Long Ditch 10Cc
St. John's Street, Spittlefields 6Bb
St. Laurence Jewry Church, Cateaton Street 5Ac
St. Laurence Pountney Churchyard, St. Laurence Pountney Lane 13Ba
St. Laurence's Alley, Cateaton Street 5Ac
St. Leonard's Church, Foster Lane 4Cc
St. Leonard's Eastcheap Churchyard, Fish Street Hill 13Ba
St. Leonard's Shoreditch Church 6Aa
St. Luke's Church, in Old Street 5Aa
St. Luke's Churchyard, Ironmonger Row 5Aa
St. Magnus Church, near London Bridge 13Bb
St. Margaret Patten's Church, Rood Lane 13Ca
St. Margaret's Chapel and Burying Ground, Chapel Street 18Ca
St. Margaret's Church, Broad Sanctuary 19Aa
St. Margaret's Church, Lothbury 13Ba
St. Margaret's Hill, in the Borough 13Ac
St. Margaret's Lane, Old Palace Yard 11Ac 19Aa

St. Martin's Alms Houses, Hog Lane 10Ca
St. Martin's Church, by Ludgate 12Ba
St. Martin's Churchyard, Ironmonger Lane 13Aa
St. Martin's Churchyard, School, Library, and Workhouse 11Ab
St. Martin's Court, St. Martin's Lane 11Aa
St. Martin's in the Fields Church, St. Martin's Lane 11Ab
St. Martin's le Grand, Aldersgate 4Cc
St. Martin's Lane, Canon Street 13Ba 13Bb
St. Martin's Lane, Charing Cross 11Ab 11Aa
St. Martin's Orgars Churchyard, St. Martin's Lane, Thames Street 13Ba
St. Martin's Outwitch Church, Threadneedle Street 13Ba
St. Martin's School and Workhouse 11Ab
St. Martin's Street, Leicester Fields 10Cb
St. Martin's Vintry Churchyard, Thames Street 13Aa
St. Mary Aldermary Church, in Bow Lane 13Aa
St. Mary Axe Lane, Leadenhall Street 13Ca 5Cc
St. Mary Axe, Leadenhall Hall Street 13Ca 5Cc
St. Mary Axe Warehouse 13Ca
St. Mary le Bone 1Cb
St. Mary le Bone Bason 1Cb 1Cc 2Ab 2Ac
St. Mary le Bone Burying Ground 1Bb 1Bc
St. Mary le Bone Church 1Cb
St. Mary le Bone Spring Gardens 1Cb
St. Mary Bothaw Churchyard, in Turnwheel Lane, Cannon Street 13Aa
St. Mary le Bow Church, Cheapside 13Aa
St. Mary, Church Lane, Rotherhithe 15Bc
St. Mary at Hill Church, near Billingsgate 13Ca
St. Mary Hill, Thames Street 13Cb 13Ca
St. Mary Magdalen Bermondsey Church, Barnaby Street 21Ca
St. Mary Magdalen's Church, in Old Fish Street 12Ca
St. Mary Overies Dock 13Ab
St. Mary Overies Stairs, Clink Street, Deadman's Place 13Ab
St. Mary Somerset Church, in Thames Street 12Ca
St. Mary Staining Churchyard, Staining Lane 5Ac
St. Mary Woolnoth's Church in Lombard Street 13Ba
St. Mary's Church, Abchurch Lane 13Ba
St. Mary's Church, in Aldermanbury 5Ac
St. Mary's Church, at Lambeth 19Bb
St. Mary's Church, Newington Butts 20Bb 20Cb
St. Mary's Church, in the Strand 11Ca
St. Mary's Church in Whitechapel 6Bc
St. Matthew's Church near Bethnal Green 6Ba

St. Matthew's Church Friday Street 12Ca
St. Michael Bassishaw Church, Basinghall Street 5Ac
St. Michael Royal's Church in College Hill 13Aa
St. Michael's Alley, Cornhill 13Ba
St. Michael's Church in Cornhill 13Ba
St. Michael's Church, near Crooked Lane 13Ba
St. Michael's Church, Queenhithe 13Aa
St. Michael's Church in Wood Street 5Ac
St. Michael's Lane, Great East Cheap 13Ba 13Bb
St. Mildred's Church in Bread Street 13Aa
St. Mildred's Church in the Poultry 13Aa
St. Nicholas Acon's Churchyard in Nicholas Lane 13Ba
St. Nicholas Alley, St. Nicholas Lane 13Ba
St. Nicholas Coleabby Church, Old Fish Street 12Ca
St. Nicholas Lane, Lombard Street 13Ba
St. Nicholas Olave Churchyard, Bread Street Hill 12Ca
St. Olave's Church, in Hart Street 13Ca
St. Olave's Church, in the Old Jewry 13Aa
St. Olave's Church in Tooly Street, Southwark 13Bb
St. Olave's Churchyard, St. Olave's Street 13Cc
St. Olave's Churchyard, Silver Street 5Ac
St. Olave's Street, Tooly Street 13Cc
St. Pancras Churchyard, Pancras Lane 13Aa
St. Paul's Cathedral 12Ca
St. Paul's Church, in Covent Garden 11Aa 11Ba
St. Paul's Church, Upper Shadwell 15Bb
St. Paul's School, St. Paul's Church Yard 12Ca
St. Peter ad Vincula, in the Tower 14Ab
St. Peter's Abbey, Westminster 19Aa
St. Peter's Alley, Cornhill 13Ba
St. Peter's Cheap Churchyard, Cheapside 13Aa
St. Peter's Church, in Cornhill 13Ba
St. Peter's Churchyard, near Paul's Wharf 12Ca
St. Peter's Hill, Thames Street 12Ca
St. Peter's le Poor Church, Broad Street 5Bc
St. Saviour's Burying Ground, Red Cross Street 13Ac
St. Saviour's Church, in the Borough 13Ab 13Bb
St. Saviour's Dock, Rotherhith 14Bc
St. Sepulchre's Church, near Newgate 4Bc
St. Sepulchre's Churchyard, Chick Lane 4Bc
St. Stephen's Church, in Coleman Street 5Ac
St. Stephen's Church, in Walbrook 13Aa 13Ba
St. Swithin's Church, in Cannon Street 13Ba
St. Swithin's Lane, Canon Street 13Ba
St. Thomas Apostle Churchyard, St. Thomas Apostle 13Aa

St. Thomas Apostle, Queen Street 13Aa
St. Thomas Burying Ground, St. Thomas Street 13Aa
St. Thomas's, Borough 13Bc
St. Thomas's Burying Ground 13Bc
St. Thomas's Church, St. Thomas's Street, Southwark 13Bc 13Bb
St. Thomas's Hospital, in the Borough, Southwark 13Bb 13Bc
St. Thomas's Street, Drury Lane 3Bc
St. Thomas's Street, Southwark 13Bc
St. Vedast, alias St. Foster's Church, Foster Lane, Cheapside 12Ca
Salisbury Court, Fleet Street 12Ba
Salisbury Court, Salisbury Square 12Aa
Salisbury Lane, Rotherhithe 22Ba 14Bc
Salisbury Square, Salisbury Court, 12Ba 12Aa
Salisbury Stairs near the Strand 11Bb
Salisbury Street, Rotherhithe 22Ca 14Cc
Salisbury Street, in the Strand 11Bb
Salisbury Walk, Chelsea Road, near Buckingham House 18Aa
Salmons Lane, near White Horse Street, Ratcliff 16Ba 16Ca
Salters Hall Court, St. Swithin's Lane 13Ba
Salters' Hall, St. Swithins Lane, Cannon Street 13Ba
Saltpetre Bank, East Smithfield and Rosemary Lane 14Bb 14Ba
Salutation Court, St. Giles's Broadway 3Ac
Sambrugh's Court, Basinghall Street 5Ac
Sandwich Court, Houndsditch 5Cc
Sandy's Street, Widegate Street 5Cc
Saracen's Head Inn, Aldgate 14Aa
Saracen's Head Inn, Camomile Street 5Cc
Saracen's Head Inn, Friday Street 12Ca
Saracen's Head Inn, Snow Hill 4Bc
Sardinian Chapel, Lincoln's Inn Fields 11Ba
Sarn Alley, Rotherhithe Wall 15Ac
Satchell's Rents, Whitecross Street 5Ab
Savage Gardens Tower Hill 14Aa
Saville Row, near New Bond Street 10Aa
Savory Mill Stairs, Rotherhithe Wall 14Bc
Savoy Alley, Savoy 11Ba
Savoy Stairs 11Bb
Savoy, in the Strand 11Bb 11Ba
Sawyers Yard, Tower Street 13Cb
Sayers Yard, Hosier Lane 4Bc
Scalding Alley, Poultry 13Ba 13Aa

School, Church Lane, Rotherhithe 15Bc
School, Dorset Street 12Ba
School, Fox and Knot Court, Cow Lane 4Bc
School, General Steward's 9Cb
School, Heneage Lane, Duke's Place 13Ca
School House Lane, Aylesberry Street 4Bb
School House Lane, Brook's Street 15Ca
School House Yard, School House Lane 15Ca
School House Yard, Sutton Street, St. John's Street 4Bb
School, Lambeth, Back Lane 19Bb
School Lane, Jamaica Street 15Bc
School, Rose Alley, East Smithfield 14Bb
School, near St. James's Church, Piccadilly 10Bb
Sclater Street, Brick Lane 6Ab
Scollop Court, Creed Lane 12Ba 12Ca
Score's Alley, Swan Alley, East Smithfield 14Bb
Scotland Yard, Whitehall 11Ab
Scots Hall, Fleet Ditch 12Ba
Scot's Wharf, Whitefriers 12Aa
Scot's Yard, Bush Lane 13Aa
Scroop's Court, Holbourn Hill 4Bc
Scrub's Square, Upper Ground 12Bb
Sea Alley, King Street, Westminster 11Ac
Seacoal Lane, Snow Hill 4Bc
Searl's Street, Lincoln's Inn Fields 3Cc 11Ca
Searl's Wharf, near Whitefriers 12Aa
Second Postern, London Wall 5Ac
Sedgwick's Rents, London Wall 5Bc
Seething Lane, Tower Street 13Ca 13Cb
Sepulchre's Alley, Giltspur Street 4Bc
Serjeants Inn, Chancery Lane 12Aa
Serjeants Inn Court, Fleet Street 12Aa
Sermon Lane, Limehouse 16Ba 16Ca
Sermon Lane, Little Carter Lane 12Ca
Serpentine River, part of 9Ab 9Ac
Sessions House, Old Bailey 4Bc
Seven Star Alley, Ratcliff Highway 15Ab
Seven Star Alley, Whitecross Street 5Ab
Seven Star Alley, Rosemary Lane 14Bb 14Ba
Seven Star Court, Great Garden, St. Catharine's Lane 14Ab
Seven Star Court, Moor Lane 5Ab
Seven Star Court, Seven Star Alley, Radcliff Highway 15Ab
Seven Step Alley, Petticoat Lane 6Ac
Seven Step Alley, Rotherhithe Wall 15Ac 23Aa
Seven Steps Yard, Gravel Lane, Hounds Ditch 6Ac

Seymour's Court, Little Shandois Street 11Ab
Shad Thames, near St. Saviour's Dock 14Ac 14Bc
Shadwell Dock, Lower Shadwell 15Bb
Shadwell Dock Stairs, near Shadwell Dock 15Cb
Shadwell Market, Middle Shadwell 15Bb
Shadwell, Wapping 15Cb
Shafts Court, Leadenhall Street 13Ca
Shakespear's Walk, Upper Shadwell 15Bb
Sharp's Alley, Cowcross 4Bc
Sharp's Buildings, Duke's Place 13Ca
Shaw's Court, near St. George's Church 13Ac
Sheep Pens, West Smithfield 4Bc
Sheer Lane, Templebar 11Ca 12Aa
Sheering's Alley, Shoreditch 6Ab
Sheers Alley, East Smithfield 14Bb
Sheers Alley, Wentworth Street 6Bc
Sheers Alley, White Street 13Ac
Sheers Alley, Wood Street 5Ac
Sheffield Street, Vere Street, Clare Market 11Ca
Shepherd and Dog Stairs, Rotherhithe 16Ab
Shepherd's Alley, Thames Street 13Aa
Shepherds Court, Little (or Upper) Brooks Street 9Ba
Shepherd's Gardens, Minories 14Aa
Shepherd's Market, near Curzon Street 9Cb
Shepherd's Mewse, Park Street 9Ba
Shepherd's Street, Oxford Street 10Aa
Sherborn Lane, Lombard Street 13Ba
Sherwood Street, near Golden Square 10Ba
Ship Alley, Broad Street, Ratcliff 15Cb
Ship Alley, Fore Street, Limehouse 16Cb
Ship Alley, Narrow Street, Limehouse 16Bb
Ship Alley, Ratcliff Highway, and Well Close Square 14Cb
Ship Court, Goat Alley, Whitecross Street 5Ab
Ship Court, in the Old Bailey 12Ba
Ship, Grange Road 22Aa
Ship Inn, Borough 13Bb
Ship Street, King Street, New Gravel Lane 15Ab
Ship Yard, Bartholomew Lane 13Ba
Ship Yard, Bishopsgate Street 5Cb
Ship Yard, Glasshouse Yard, near Aldersgate Bars 4Cb
Ship Yard, Petty France 18Ba
Ship Yard, Redcross Street 5Ac
Ship Yard, without Temple Bar 11Ca
Shipping Stairs, Limehouse 16Bb
Shoe Lane, in Fleet Street 4Bc 4Ac 12Ba

Shoemaker Row, Aldgate 14Aa 13Ca
Shoemaker Row, Blackfriers 12Ba
Shooter's Court, Basinghall Street 5Ac
Shoreditch Alley, Shoreditch 6Ab
Shorter's Court, Throckmorton Street 13Ba
Short's Garden's, Drury Lane 11Aa 3Ac
Shoulder of Mutton Alley, Limehouse 16B
Shovel Alley, Great Gardens, St. Catharine's Lane 14Bb
Shovel Alley, Wood Street 5Ac
Shrewsbury's Court, Whitecross Street 5Ab
Shug Lane, near Piccadilly 10Cb 10Bb 10Ba
Sidney Street, Leicester Fields 10Ca
Silver Court, Woodstock Street 9Ca
Silver Street, Bloomsbury Market 3Bc
Silver Street, near Golden Square 10Ba
Silver Street, Green Alley, Tooly Street 13Bc
Silver Street, Hare Street 6Bb
Silver Street, King Street, New Gravel Lane 15Ab
Silver Street, Lombard Street, Whitefriers 12Aa
Silver Street, Pelham Street 6Bb
Silver Street, Wood Street 5Ac
Sing's Court, Little Michel Street 5Aa
Sion College Court, London 5Ac
Sion College, London Wall 5Ac
Sion Court, Philip Lane 5Ac
Sir John Oldcastle's, Coppice Row 4Ab 4Aa
Sir William Warren's Square, Wapping Dock 15Ab 15Ac
Six Gardens Court, Paul's Alley 4Cc
Size Yard, White Chapel 6Bc
Skin Market, Bank Side 12Cb
Skin Market, Woods Close 4Ba
Skinner Street, Bishopsgate Street 5Cb
Skinners' Alms Houses, Mile End Old Town 7Bb
Skinners' Hall, on Dowgate Hill 13Aa
Skinners' Rent, Perriwinkle Street 16Aa
Slaughter House Yard, Channel Row 11Ac
Slaughter House Yard, Fashion Street 5Ac
Slaughter House Yard, Turnmill Street 4Bb
Slaughter's Court, Blue Anchor Alley 14Ba
Sleep's Alley, Islington Road, St. John's Street 4Ba
Sluice Street, near Wright Street, Rotherhithe 16Ab
Smallcoal Alley, Fashion Street 6Bc
Smallcoal Alley, near Primrose Street, Bishopsgate Street 5Cb
Smart's Key, Thames Street 13Cb
Smithfield Bars, Porters Block 4Bc

Smith's Alley, Joiners Street 13Bb
Smith's Alley, Ropemakers Field, Limehouse 16Cb
Smith's Court, Aldersgate Street 4Cc
Smith's Court, Fashion Street 6Ac
Smith's Court, Windmill Street 10Ba 10Ca
Smith's Passage in the Curtain 5Cb
Smith's Rents, Bank Side 13Ab
Smith's Rents, Barnaby Street 13Cc
Smith's Rents, Petty France, Westminster 18Ba
Smith's Rents, St. John's Street 4Bb
Smith's Street, Marsham Street 18Ca
Smock Alley, Petticoat Lane 6Ac
Sneads Court, Brick Street 9Cb
Snow Hill, Holbourn Bridge 4Bc
Snow's Fields, Barnaby Street 13Bc
Snuff Yard, Houndsditch 5Cc
Soap Yard, Harrow Corner 13Ab
Soho 10Ca
Soho Square, near Oxford Street 2Cc 10Ca
Somers Street, Hockley in the Hole 4Ab
Somerset House, Strand 11Ba
Somerset Stairs, Somerset House 11Ca
Somerset Street, Whitechapel 14Aa
Somerset Water Gate 11Ba
Somerset Watergate Stairs 11Bb
Sopers Alley, Whitecross Street 5Ab
South Moulton Row, David Street 9Ca
South Sea Court, Lombard Street 12Cc
South Sea House, Threadneedle Street 13Ba
South Sea Passage, Broad Street 13Ba
South Sea Yard, Threadneedle Street 13Ba
South Street, Audley Street 9Bb
South Street, Spittle Fields Market 6Ac
Southampton Buildings, Chancery Lane 3Cc
Southampton Row, near Queen Square 3Ab 3Bb
Southampton Street, Covent Garden and the Strand 11Ba
Southampton Street, High Holbourn 3Bc
Spicer Street, Brick Lane, Spittlefields 6Bb
Spinners Yard, Windmill Hill 5Bb
Spittle Fields Market, Crispen Street 6Ac
Spittle Square, Bishopsgate Street 6Ab 5Cb
Spittle Street, Spicer Street, Spittlefields 6Bb
Spread Eagle Court, Church Lane, Rotherith 15Bc
Spread Eagle Court, Gray's Inn Lane 4Ac
Spread Eagle Court, Kingsland Road 5Ca

Spread Eagle Court, Threadneedle Street 13Ba
Spread Eagle Inn, Grace Church Street 13Ba
Spring Garden Chappel 11Ab
Spring Garden, Charing Cross 10Cb 11Ab
Spring Garden Mewse, Spring Garden, Charing Cross 11Ab
Spring Gardens, Bull Lane, Stepney 8Ac
Spring Street, Middle Shadwell 15Bb
Spur Inn, Borough 13Ac
Spur Street, Leicester Fields 10Cb
Staining Lane, Maiden Lane 5Ac 4Cc
Stamford's Buildings, Ragged Row, Old Street 4Cb
Stamp Office, Lincolns Inn 3Cc
Stangate Stairs, Lambeth 19Ba
Stangate Street, Lambeth 19Ba
Stanhope Street, Clare Street, Clare Market 11Ba 11Ca
Stansbury Court, Piccadilly 10Bb
Staple's Court, Beek Street 10Ba
Staple's Inn, Holbourn 4Ac
Star Alley, Barnaby Street 13Cc
Star Alley, East Smithfield 14Bb
Star Alley, Fenchurch Street 13Ca
Star Court, Bread Street 13Aa
Star Court, Butcher Row 11Ca
Star Court, Cheapside 12Ca
Star Court, Compton Street 10Ca
Star Court, Cross Lane, Parker's Lane 3Bc
Star Court, Great East Cheap 13Ba
Star Court, Grub Street 5Ac
Star Court, London Wall 5Bc
Star Court, Minories 14Aa
Star Court, Old Fish Street 12Ca
Star Inn, Fish Street Hill 13Ba
Star Street, Wapping 15Bb
Star Yard, Huggin Lane 13Aa
Star Yard, Moor Lane 5Ac
Starch Alley, Rotten Row, Goswell Street 4Cb
Starch Yard, Back Lane, Lambeth 19Bb
Starch Yard, Seven Stars Alley, Radcliff Highway 15Ab
Stationers' Court, Ave Mary Lane 12Ba 12Ca
Stationer's Hall, near Ludgate Street 12Ba
Steedwell Street, Hog Lane 11Aa 10Ca
Steel Yard Stairs, Steel Yard Wharf, Thames Street 13Ab
Steel Yard, Steel Yard Wharf 13Ab
Steel Yard Wharf, near Dowgate Wharf 13Ab
Steel's Court, Bread Street 13Aa

Steeps Gardens, Kent Street 21Ba
Stepney Causeway, Whitehorse Lane 15Ca
Stepney Green, Stepney 8Ac 7Cc
Stepney, near Mile End 8Ac
Stepney Rents, Shoreditch 6Aa
Steven's Alley, Channel Row 11Ac
Steward Street, Spittlefields 6Ac
Steward's Court, Clerkenwell Green 4Bb
Steward's Rents, Great Wild Street 11Ba
Still Alley, Bishopsgate Street 5Cc
Still Alley, George Street 7Aa
Still Alley, New Street, St. Thomas's 13Bc
Still Alley, near Sun Alley, Houndsditch 5Cc
Still Stairs, Pickle Herring Street 14Ac
Stitchbone's Court, High Holbourn 3Cc
Stockingframe Alley, Shoreditch 5Cb
Stone Alley, Broad Street, Ratcliff 16Aa
Stone Court, Aldersgate Street 4Cc
Stone Court, Fetter Lane 4Ac
Stone Court, St. Catherine's 14Bb 14Bc
Stone House Yard, near Great Stone Stairs 15Cb
Stone Stairs, near Ratcliff Cross 16Ab
Stone Yard, Tooly Street 13Bb
Stonecutters Alley, Black Friars and Fleet Ditch 12Ba
Stonecutters Alley, Little Queen Street 3Bc
Stonecutters Alley, Pall Mall 10Cb
Stonecutters Court, Old Street 5Aa
Stonecutters Street, Shoe Lane 4Bc
Stonecutters Yard, Butcher Row, Radcliff 16Aa
Stonecutters Yard, near Castle Street 10Ba
Stonecutters Yard, near Castle Street 13Ab
Stonecutters Yard, Kent Street 21Aa
Stonecutters Yard, Peter Street 18Ca
Stonecutters Yard, Poor Jewry Lane 14Aa
Stone's Rents, near the Rope Walk, Limehouse 16Ba
Stoney Lane, Petticoat Lane 6Ac
Stoney Lane, St. Olaves Street 13Cb 13Cc
Stoney Street, near Deadman's Place 13Ab
Store House Yard 14Bb
Story's Gate, Delahay Street 10Cc
Strafford Street, Albemarle Street 10Ab
Strand Bridge Stairs 11Ca
Strand Bridge, Strand Lane 11Ca
Strand, Charing Cross to Temple Bar 11Ba 11Ab 11Bb
Strand Lane in the Strand 11Bc

Strangeways Street, Saffron Hill 4Bb 4Ab
Stretton Grounds, Westminster 18Ca
Stretton Street, Piccadilly 10Ab
Stripes Yard, Pettycoat Lane 6Ac
Stroud's Court, Leather Lane 4Ab
Strumbelo, Chelsea 17Bb 17Cb
Stut's Alley, Kent Street 21Aa
Suffolk Lane, Thames Street 13Ba
Suffolk Street, in the Mint 12Cc
Sugar Baker's Yard, King Street, near Leadenhall Street 13Ca
Sugar House Yard, Watch House, Ratcliff 16Aa
Sugar Loaf Alley, Barnaby Street 13Cc
Sugar Loaf Alley, Garlick Hill 13Aa
Sugar Loaf Alley, Portpool Lane 4Ab
Sugar Loaf Court, Angel Alley, Bishopsgate Street 5Cc
Sugar Loaf Court, Catharine Wheel Alley 6Bc
Sugar Loaf Court, Dorset Street 12Ba
Sugar Loaf Court, Goodman's Yard 14Aa
Sugar Loaf Court, Lamb Alley, Bishopsgate Street 5Cc
Sugar Loaf Court, Leadenhall Street 13Ca
Sugar Loaf Court, Little Elbow Lane 13Aa
Sugar Loaf Court, Moor Lane 5Ac
Sugar Loaf Court, Peter Street, Hick's Hall 4Bb
Sugar Loaf Court, Wentworth Street 6Ac
Sun Alley, Chick Lane 4Bc
Sun Alley, Cowcross 4Bb
Sun Alley, East Smithfield 14Bb
Sun Alley, Golden Lane 5Ab
Sun Alley, Grub Street 5Ab
Sun Alley, Houndsditch 5Cc
Sun Alley, King Street, Cheapside 13Aa
Sun Court, Cornhill 13Ba
Sun Court, Petticoat Lane 6Ac
Sun Court, Threadneedle Street 13Ba
Sun Court, White Chapel 14Aa
Sun Court, Wood Street 5Ac
Sun and Gun Yard, Narrow Street, Limehouse 16Bb
Sun Street, Bishopsgate Street 5Cc
Sun Tavern Fields, near Upper Shadwell 15Ba
Sun Yard, Bishopsgate Street, near the
Old South Sea House 13Ca 5Cc
Sun Yard, Nightingale Lane 14Bb
Surrey Stairs, Surrey Street 11Ca
Surrey Street, in the Strand 11Ca
Sutton Street, Hog Lane, Soho 2Cc

Sutton Street, St. John's Street 4Bb
Sutton's Court, Bishopsgate Street 5Cc
Sutton's Court, Holbourn Hill 4Bc
Swan Alley, Barnaby Street 21Ca
Swan Alley, Coleman Street 5Bc
Swan Alley, East Smithfield 14Bb
Swan Alley, Golden Lane 5Ab
Swan Alley, Goswel Street 4Cb
Swan Alley, near Hanover Street, Rotherhithe 15Bc
Swan Alley, Minories 14Aa
Swan Alley, Puddle Dock Hill 12Ba
Swan Alley, near Ratcliff Cross 16Aa
Swan Alley, Wardour Street 10Ca
Swan Court, Grub Street 5Ab
Swan Court, Narrow Wall 11Cb
Swan Court, Petticoat Lane 6Ac
Swan Court, Swan Alley, East Smithfield 14Bb
Swan Inn, Holbourn Bridge 4Bc
Swan Street, New Cock Lane 6Ab
Swan and Two Necks Inn, Lad Lane 5Ac
Swan and Two Necks Inn, St. John's Street 4Bb
Swan and Two Necks Stable Yard, Tothil Street 18Ca
Swan Yard, Church Street, Lambeth 19Bb
Swan Yard, Newgate Street 4Bc 4Cc
Swan Yard, Shoreditch 6Ab
Swan Yard, in the Strand, near Drury Lane 11Ba
Swan Yard, Townsend Lane 4Ab
Swedish Church, Princes Square 14Cb
Sweedland Court, Bishopsgate Street 5Cc
Sweedland Court, Little Tower Hill 14Ab
Sweet's Court, Trinity Lane 13Aa
Sweet Apple Court, Dunning's Alley 5Cc
Sweetings Passage, Moor Lane 5Ac
Swithin's Alley, Threadneedle Street 13Ba
Swithin's Rents, Threadneedle Street 13Ba
Sword and Buckler Court, Ludgate Hill 12Ba
Sycamore Yard, Kent Street 21Aa
Symond's Inn, Chancery Lane 4Ac
Syths Lane, near Queen Street 13Aa

Tabernacle Yard, Wheeler Street 6Ab
Talbot Court, Gracechurch Street 0313Ba
Talbot Court, Portpool Lane 4Ab
Talbot Inn, Borough 13Ac
Talbot Inn, Surrey Street, Strand 11Ca

Talbot Inn, Whitechapel 14Ba
Tallow Chandler's Hall, Dowgate Hill 13Aa
Tan Alley, Godder's Rents, Wheeler Street 6Ab
Tanfield Court, Inner Temple 12Aa
Tanner's Row, Montague Street 6Bc
Tanner's Yard 21Ba 21Ca 14Ac
Tarres Wharf, Durham Yard 11Bb
Tart Court, Pye Corner, West Smithfield 4Bc 4Cc
Tash Street, Gray's Inn Lane 4Ab 3Cb
Tattle Street, Little Gray's Inn Lane 3Cb 4Ab
Tavistock Court, Tavistock Street 11Ba
Tavistock Street, Southampton Street, Covent Garden 11Ba
Taylor's Court, Bow Lane 13Aa
Teed's Yard, Worcester Street 13Ac
Temple 12Aa
Temple Bar, Fleet Street 12Aa
Temple Church, Inner Temple Lane 12Aa
Temple Key, Thames Street 13Cb
Temple Lane, Whitefriers 12Aa
Temple Mewse, Great Friers Gate, Fleet Street 12Aa
Temple Stairs, Temple Lane 12Aa
Temple Street, Whitefriers 12Aa
Ten Bell Court, Snow Hill 4Bc
Ten Feet Way, Nightingale Lane 14Bb 14Cb
Tenderdown Street, Hanover Square 10Aa
Tennis Court, Church Entry, Shoemaker Row 12Ba
Tennis Court, High Holbourn 3Bc
Tennis Court, Middle Row, Holbourn 4Ac
Tenter Alley, Little Moorfields 5Bc 5Ac
Tenter Alley, Tooly Street 13Bc
Tents, near Maze Pond 13Bc
Terras Walk, York Buildings 11Bb
Thames Street, near London
Bridge 12Ba 12Ca 13Aa 13Bb 13Cb
Thatch'd Alley, Chick Lane 4Bc
Thatch'd House Alley, in the Strand 11Ab 11Bb
Thatch'd House Court, St. James's Street 10Bb
Thavies Inn, by St. Andrew's Church, Holbourn 4Ac
Theatre Royal, Covent Garden 11Ba
Theiving Lane, King's Street, Westminster 11Ac
Theobald's Court, in the Strand 11Bb
Theobald's Court, Theobald's Row 3Bb
Theobald's Row, Red Lion Street 3Bc 3Bb 3Cb
Thomas Street, Bacon Street, Shoreditch Fields 6Bb
Thomas Street, Gainsford Street 14Ac

Thomas's Rents, Fore Street, Limehouse 16Cb
Thomas's Street, Virginia Row, near Greyhound Lane 6Cb
Thompson's Rents, Halfmoon Alley 5Cc
Thompson's Rents, London Wall 5Bc
Thral Street, Spitlefields 6Bc
Threadneedle Street, Bishopsgate Street 13Ba
Three Bowl Alley, Long Alley, Moorfields 5Cb
Three Bowl Court, Houndsditch 14Aa
Three Colt Alley, Cinnamon Street 15Ab
Three Colt Corner St. John's Street 6Bb
Three Colt Lane, Hare Street 6Bb
Three Colt Street, Limehouse 16Ca
Three Colt Yard, Hart Street, Crutched Friars 13Ca
Three Colt Yard, London Wall 5Bc
Three Colt Yard, Mile End 7Cb
Three Compasses Court, near Brook Street 15Ca 8Aa
Three Coney Walk, Lambeth 19Cb
Three Crane Court in the Borough 13Ac
Three Crane Lane, Thames Street 13Aa 13Ab
Three Crane Stairs, Queen Street 13Ab
Three Cranes, Thames Street 13Ab
Three Crown Court in the Borough 13Ab
Three Crown Court, Foster Lane 4Cc
Three Crown Court, Garlick Hill 13Aa
Three Crown Court, Old Castle Street 6Ac
Three Crown Court, Poor Jewry Lane 14Aa
Three Crown Court, Wheeler Street 6Ab
Three Cup Alley, Dean Street 15Cb
Three Cup Alley, Shoreditch 5Cb
Three Cup Yard, Bedford Street 3Cc
Three Cups Inn, Bread Street 13Aa
Three Cups Inn, High Holbourn 3Cc
Three Cups Inn, Pickaxe Street 4Cb
Three Cups Inn, St. John's Street 4Bb
Three Daggers Court, Fore Street 5Ac
Three Daggers Court, Old Change 12Ca
Three Falcons Court, Fleet Street 12Aa
Three Falcons Court, St. Margaret's Hill 13Ac
Three Fox Court, Long Lane 4Cc
Three Fox Court, Narrow Street, Radcliff 16Aa 16Ab
Three Hammer Alley, Silver Street, near Tooly Street 13Bc
Three Herring Court, Red Cross Street 5Ab
Three Horseshoes Court, Angel Court, Snow Hill 12Bc
Three Horseshoes Court, Giltspur Street 4Bc
Three Horseshoes Court, White Cross Street 5Ab 5Ac

Three Horseshoes Yard, James Street 9Ca
Three King Court, Fleet Street 12Aa
Three King Court, King Street, Covent Garden 11Aa
Three King Court, Lombard Street 13Ba
Three King Court, Minories 14Aa
Three King Yard, David Street 9Ca
Three Kings Inn, Piccadilly 10Ab
Three Leg Alley, East Harding Street 4Ac
Three Leg Court, Whitecross Street 5Ac
Three Link Alley, Fashion Street 6Bc
Three Mariners Stair, Rotherhithe 14Cc
Three Nun Court, Threadneedle Street 13Ba
Three Nuns Yard, Whitechapel 14Aa
Three Pigeon Court, Long Alley, Moorfields 5Cb
Three Slipper Court, Hand Alley, Bishopsgate Street 5Cc
Three Step Alley, Rotherhithe 15Ac
Three Still Court, Bishopsgate Street 5Cc
Three Tun Alley, Bishopsgate Street 5Cc
Three Tun Alley, London Wall 5Bc
Three Tun Alley, Petticoat Lane 6Ac
Three Tun Alley, St. Margaret's Hill 13Ac
Three Tun Alley, Thames Street 13Bb
Three Tun Court, Brown Street 5Ab
Three Tun Court, College Court, Nightingale Lane 14Bb
Three Tun Court, Hart Street, Crutched Friars 13Ca
Three Tun Court, Little Moorgate, London Wall 5Bc
Three Tun Court, Old Castle Street 6Ac
Three Tun Court, Redcross Street 5Ab
Three Tun Court, St. Michael's Lane 13Bb
Three Tun Court, Wentworth Street 6Ac
Thrift Street, Soho 10Ca
Throgmorton Street, Lothbury 13Ba
Thumbyard, Sutton Street 4Bb
Tichfield Street, Chapel Street 2Cc
Tichfield Street, Margaret Street 2Bc
Tiger Court, Whitecross Street 5Ab
Tindal's Burying Ground, Royal Row 5Bb 5Ab
Tinder Box Court, White Lion Yard, Norton Falgate 6Ab
Tite's Alley, Limehouse 16Cb
Titmouse Alley, Farmer Street 15Bb
Titus Court, Union Court, Holbourn Hill 4Bc
Tobacco Pipe Alley, Sun Yard, Nightingale Lane 14Bb
Tobacco Pipe Yard, Old Gravel Lane 15Ab
Tobacco Roll Court, Long Alley, Moorfields 5Bc
Tokenhouse Yard, Lothbury 5Bc 13Ba

Tom's Yard, Whitechapel 6Cc
Tongs Yard, Whitechapel 6Cc
Tooly Stairs, Tooly Street 13Bb
Tooly Street, Southwark 13Bb
Tooly's Gate, Tooly Street 13Cc
Tooly's Water Gate, near Tooly Street 13Bb
Torment Hill, Broad Way 18Ca
Tothill Fields, Westminster 18Bb
Tothill Street, Westminster 18Ca
Tottenham Court Road, St. Giles's 2Cc 2Cb 2Bb
Tottenham Court, Tottenham Court Road 2Cc
Tower Dock, near the Tower 13Cb
Tower Hill 14Ab
Tower Hill Passage, Little Tower Hill 14Ab
Tower Royal Court, Tower Royal 13Aa
Tower Royal, near St. Thomas Apostle 13Aa
Tower Stairs, Tower 13Cb
Tower Street, Little Earl Street, Seven Dials 11Aa
Tower Wharf 14Ab
Townditch, Christ's Hospital 4Cc
Townsend Lane, Hockley in the Hole 4Ab
Townsend Lane, Thames Street 13Aa
Traitors Bridge, The Tower 14Ab
Treasury, Whitehall 11Ac
Trig Lane, Thames Street 12Ca
Trig Stairs, Trig Lane 12Ca
Trinity Alms Houses, Mile End Old Town 7Bb
Trinity Church, Little Minories 14Aa
Trinity Court, Aldersgate Street 4Cc
Trinity Court, Little Minories 14Aa
Trinity Court, Little Trinity Lane 13Aa
Trinity House, Water Lane Tower Street 13Cb
Trinity Lane, Garlick Hill 13Aa
Trinity Passage 15Ca
Trinity Stairs, near Ship Alley, Broad Street 15Cb
Trinity Street, Rotherhithe 16Bc
Trotman's Free School, Brown Street 5Ab
Trotter Alley, Barnaby Street 13Cc
Trotter Bone Alley, Duke Street 12Cc
Trump Alley, Cheapside 13Aa
Trump Street, King Street 13Aa
Tryance Court, Red Lion Street 6Ac
Trype Yard, Dunnings Alley, Bishopsgate Street 5Cc
Type Yard, Petticoat Lane 6Ac
Tudor Street, Bridewell Precinct 12Ba

Tufton Street, Vine Street, Westminster 19Aa
Tukes Court, Cursitars Alley, Chancery Lane 4Ac
Turks Row, Chelsea 17Ac
Turnabout Alley, Windmill Hill Row 5Bb
Turnagain Lane, Snow Hill 4Bc
Turnagain Lane, Thomas Street 6Cb
Turner's Alley, Little Eastcheap 13Ca
Turner's Court, St. Martin's Lane 11Ab
Turner's Hall, on College Hill 13Aa
Turnmill Street, Cow Cross 4Bb
Turnpike, Hyde Park Corner 9Bc
Turnpike, Kent Road, near the Greyhound 22Ab 22Ac
Turnpike, Mile End New Town 7Bc
Turnpike, Newington Butts 20Ca
Turnpike, Tottenham Court 2Ba 2Bb
Turnpike, by Tyburn 9Aa
Turnstile Alley, Drury Lane 11Ba
Turnwheel Lane, Canon Street 13Aa
Turville Street, New Cock Lane 6Aa 6Ab
Tuthill Court, Tuthill Street 18Ca
Tuttle Court, Barnaby Street 13Cc
Tweezers Alley, Milford Lane 11Ca
Twelve Bell Court, Bow Lane 13Aa
Twisters Alley, Chequer Alley, Whitecross Street 5Ab
Two Brewers Yard, near Monmouth Street 11Aa
Two Swans Inn, Bishopsgate Street 5Cc
Twyford's Alley, Petty France 18Ca
Tyburn 9Aa
Tyburn House 9Aa
Tyburn Lane, Hide-park Road 9Aa 9Ba 9Bb 9Cb 9Cc
Tyburn Road, Oxford Street 9Aa 9Ba 9Ca
Tyers's Gate, Barnaby Street 13Cc
Tyler's Court 18Ba
Tyler's Street, King Street, near Carnaby Market 10Ba
Tyson's Street, Church Street 6Ba

Unicorn Court, Haymarket 10Cb
Unicorn Court, Kent Street 13Ac
Unicorn Court, Redcross Street 14Bb
Unicorn Yard, Blackman Street 20Ca 21Aa
Unicorn Yard, St. Olave's Street 13Cc
Union Court, Broad Street 5Cc
Union Court, Scroop's Court, Holbourn Hill 4Ac 4Bc
Union Court, Wormwood Street 5Cc
Union Fire Office, Gutter Lane 4Cc

Union Stairs, Wapping 14Cc
Union Street, King Street 11Ac
Union Street, New Bond Street 10Aa
Upper Brook Street, Grosvenor Square 9Ba
Upper Grosvenor Street, Grosvenor Square 9Ba
Upper Ground, near the Green Walk 12Bb
Upper Middle Row, Broad St. Giles's 3Ac
Upper Moorfields 5Bb
Upper Shadwell, Ratcliff Highway 15Bb 15Cb
Upper Turnstile, High Holbourn 3Bc
Upper Wet Dock, near Deptford 24Bb

Valiant Soldier Alley, Barnaby Street 13Cc
Vaux Hall, near Lambeth 19Bc
Vaux Hall, Spring Garden 19Bc
Vaux Hall Stairs, Vaux Hall 19Ac 19Bc
Venetian Chapel, Dean Street, Soho 10Ca
Vere Street, Clare Market 11Ba 11Ca
Vere Street, Oxford Street 1Cc
Victualling Office, Tower Hill 14Bb
Vigo Lane, Burlington Gardens 10Ab 10Bb
Villars Court, St. James's Street 10Bb
Villars Street, in the Strand 11Ab
Vine Court, Bishopsgate Street 5Cc
Vine Court, Golden Lane 5Ab
Vine Court, Gravel Lane 5Cc
Vine Court, Harp Alley, Shoe Lane 4Bc
Vine Court, Moor Lane 5Ac
Vine Court, Narrow Street 16Bb
Vine Court, Onslow Street, Vine Street 4Ab
Vine Court, Vine Street 6Ab
Vine Court, Vine Yard, St. Olave's Street 13Cc
Vine Court, White Chapel 6Cc
Vine Inn, Bishopsgate Street 5Cc
Vine Street, Broad St. Giles's 3Ac
Vine Street, Hatton Wall 4Ab
Vine Street, Lamb Street 6Ab
Vine Street, Millbank 19Aa
Vine Street, Minories 14Aa
Vine Street, Narrow Wall 11Cc 12Ac
Vine Street, Shandos Street 11Ab
Vine Street, Warwick Street 10Bb 10Ba
Vine Yard, Pick Ax Street 4Cb
Vine Yard, St. Olaves Street 13Cc 13Cb
Vine Yard, near the Watch House, Radcliff 16Aa

Vinegar Yard, Barnaby Street 13Cc
Vinegar Yard, Crown Alley, Broad St. Giles 3Ac
Vinegar Yard, Drury Lane 11Ba
Vinegar Yard, George Street 12Cc
Vinegar Yard, Sun Yard, Nightingale Lane 14Bb
Vintners' Alms Houses, Mile End Old Town 7Bb
Vintners' Hall, in Thames Street 13Aa
Virginia Court, Artichoke Lane 14Cb
Virginia Court, Recross Street, Butcher Row 14Bb
Virginia Planter Hill, Upper Shadwell 15Cb
Virginia Row, Castle Street, Shoreditch 6Aa
Virginia Row, Greyhound Lane 6Cb 7Ab
Virginia Street, Ratcliff Highway 14Cb

Walbrook, near Dowgate Hill 13Aa
Walbrook Lane, Stocks Market 13Aa
Walker's Court, Knaves Acre 10Ca
Wall's Alley, Minories 14Aa
Walnut Tree Alley, Bishopsgate Street 5Cc
Walnut Tree Court, Tooley Street 13Bb
Waltons Court, Church Yard Alley 14Bb
Wapping 15Ac 15Bb
Wapping Dock Stairs, Wapping Dock Street 15Ac
Wapping Dock Street, Wapping Dock 15Ac
Wapping New Stairs, Wapping 15Ac
Wapping Old Stairs, Wapping 14Cc
Wapping Street, Hermitage 14Cc 15Ac
Warden's Court, Clerkenwell Close 4Ab 4Bb
Wardour Street, Oxford Street 10Ca 10Ba 2Bc
Wardrobe Court, Great Carter Lane 12Ca
Ward's Court, Goswell Street 4Cb
Warner's Yard, Mincing Lane 13Ca
Warnford Court, Throgmorton Street 13Ba
Warwick Court, Berry Street 10Bb 5Bc
Warwick Court, High Holbourn 3Cc
Warwick Court, Warwick Lane 4Bc 4Cc
Warwick Court, Warwick Street, Charing Cross 10Cb
Warwick Lane, Newgate Street 4Cc 12Ca
Warwick Street, Cockspur Street 10Cb
Warwick Street, near Golden Square 10Ba
Watch House, Aldersgate Bars 4Cb
Watch House, Broad Sanctuary 19Aa
Watch House, Butcher Row, Ratcliff 16Aa
Watch House, Clerkenwell 4Bb
Watch House, Cold Bath 4Ab

Watch House, High Holbourn 3Bc
Watch House, Holbourn Bars 4Ac
Watch House, Redcross Street 5Ab
Watch House, near Shoreditch Church 6Aa
Watch House, Strand 11Ba
Water House Lane, Lower Shadwell 15Cb
Water House, Red Cross Alley, London Bridge 13Bb
Water Lane, Fleet Street 12Aa
Water Lane, Mill Street 14Bc
Water Lane, Tower Street 13Cb
Water Street, Arundel Street, Strand 11Ca
Water Street, Blackfriers 12Ba
Water Street, Bridewell Precinct 12Ba
Water Works, Middle Shadwell 7Ba
Water Works, New River Head 4Aa
Water Works, Savory Mill Stairs, Rotherhithe Wall 14Bc
Water Works, York Buildings 11Bb
Waterman's Alley, New Street, St. Thomas's 13Bc
Waterman's Lane, Whitefriers 12Aa
Watermen's Hall, Cole Harbour 13Ab
Watling Street, St. Paul's Church Yard 12Ca
Watts Court, East Smithfield 14Bb
Wax Chandler's Hall, Gutter Lane 4Cc
Weavers Alley, near Spicer's Street 6Bb
Weavers and Drapers Alms Houses, at Hoxton 5Ca
Weavers' Hall, Basinghall Street 5Ac
Webb's Square, near Back Hill, Shoreditch 6Ab
Well Alley, King Street, Tooly Street 13Bb
Well Alley, Minories 14Aa
Well Alley, Wapping Dock 15Ac
Well and Bucket Alley, Old Street 5Ab
Well and Bucket Court, Old Street 5Ab
Well Court, Queen Street 13Aa
Well Court, Shoe Lane 4Bc
Well Street, East Smithfield, near
  Well Close Square 14Ba 14Bb
Well Street, Great Germain Street 10Bb
Well Street, Spittle Street 6Bb 6Bc
Well Yard, Church Yard Alley, Rosemary Lane 14Bb
Well Yard, near Little Britain 4Cc
Wellbank Street, Henrietta Street 1Cc
Wellbeck Mewse, Wellbeck Street 1Cc
Wellclose Square, Rosemary Lane 14Ca 14Cb 14Ba 14Ab
Well's Yard, Bambridge Street 2Cc

Welsh School, Clerkenwell Green 4Bb
Wentworth Street, Spitlefields 6Ac
Were Row, Red Lyon Street, White Chappel 14Ba
West Harding Street, Fetter Lane 4Ac
West Lane, Rotherhithe 23Aa
West Lane Stairs, Rotherhithe 15Ac
West Smithfield 4Bc 4Cc
West Street, Litchfield Street, Soho 11Aa
West Street, Spitlefields Market 6Ac
Westminster Abbey 19Aa
Westminster Bridge 11Bc
Westminster Bridge Stairs 11Ac
Westminster Hall Court, Dunning's Alley 5Cc
Westminster Hall, New Palace Yard 19Aa
Westminster Infirmary, Petty France 18Ba
Westmoorland Court, Bartholomew Close 4Cc
Westmoorland Court, Noble Street 5Ac
West's Gardens, New Gravel Lane 15Ab 15Bb
Whalebone Court, Throgmorton Street 13Ba
Wharton's Court, Holbourn 4Ac
Wheatsheaf Alley, Barnaby Street 13Cc
Wheatsheaf Alley, Thames Street 13Bb
Wheeler Street Chapel 6Ab
Wheeler Street, Spitlefields 6Ab
Wheelers Lane, St. Olave Street 13Cc
Wheeler's Yard, Park Gate, Southwark 13Ac
Wheeler's Yard, Wheelers Lane 13Cc
Wheelwright Yard, Nightingale Lane 14Bb
Whetster's Ground, Peter Street 18Ca
Whetston's Park, near Lincoln's Inn Fields 3Cc
Whicker's Alms Houses, Chapel Street, Westminster 18Ba
Whistler's Court, Salters Hall Court 13Ba
Whitcomb Alley, Great Queen Street 3Bc
Whitcomb Street, Hedge Lane 10Ca 10Cb
Whitcomb's Court, Hedge Lane 10Cb
White Ball Court, Castle Street 11Ab
White Bear Alley, Addle Hill 12Ca 12Ba
White Bear Alley, Kent Street 21Aa
White Bear Alley, Redcross Street 14Bb
White Bear Alley, Rosemary Lane, near the Minories 14Aa
White Bear Alley, Whitechapel 14Aa
White Bear Inn, Basinghall Street 5Ac
White Bear Inn, Piccadilly 10Cb
White Chapel 14Aa 6Bc 6Cc
White Chapel, near Aldgate 6Cc

White Chapel Alms Houses, near Hampshire Court 6Cc
White Chapel Field Gate, White Chapel 6Cc
White Cock Alley, Thames Street 13Bb
White Cross Street, Cripplegate 5Ab 5Ac
White Cross Street, Queen Street 13Ac 12Cc
White Friers Dock 12Aa
White Friers, Lombard Street, near Fleet Street 12Aa
White Friers Stairs, White Friers 12Aa
White Hart Buildings, corner of Drury Lane 3Ac
White Hart Court, Barnaby Street 13Cc
White Hart Court, Bishopsgate Street 5Cc
White Hart Court, Broad Street 16Aa
White Hart Court, Castle Street 11Ab 11Aa
White Hart Court, Leaden Hall Street 13Ca
White Hart Court, Old Street 5Ab
White Hart Inn, Borough 13Ac
White Hart Inn, Fore Street 5Ac
White Hart Inn, Long Acre 11Ba
White Hart Inn, Newington Butts 20Cb
White Hart Inn, St. John's Street 4Bb
White Hart Inn, Whitechapel 14Aa
White Hart Stairs, Lambeth 19Bb
White Hart Street, Warwick Lane 12Ca
White Hart Yard, Barnaby Street 13Cc
White Hart Yard, Drury Lane 11Ba
White Hart Yard, Gracechurch Street 13Ba
White Hart Yard, near Maudling's Rents, Lower East
  Smithfield 14Bb
White Hart Yard, Red Lion Back Court,
  Charter House Lane 4Cb 4Cc
White Hart Yard, Whitecross Street 5Ab
White Hind Court, Bishopsgate Street 5Cc
White Hind Court, Coleman Street 5Ac
White Horse Alley, Chick Lane 4Bc
White Horse Alley, Cowcross 4Bb
White Horse Alley, Fenchurch Street 13Ca
White Horse Alley, near Guy of Warwick Court,
  Upper Ground 12Bb
White Horse Alley, Turnmill Street 4Bb
White Horse Court, Addle Hill 12Ca
White Horse Court, Barnaby Street 21Ca
White Horse Court, in the Borough 13Bb
White Horse Court, Fore Street 5Bc
White Horse Court, Rosemary Lane 14Aa
White Horse Court, Whitecross Street 5Ab

White Horse Inn, Coleman Street 5Ac
White Horse Inn, Cripplegate 5Ac
White Horse Inn, Fetter Lane 4Ac
White Horse Inn, Fleet Market 4Bc
White Horse Inn, Fleet Street 12Aa
White Horse Inn, Friday Street 12Ca
White Horse Inn, London Wall 5Bc
White Horse Inn, Mile End 7Cb
White Horse Inn, Piccadilly 10Bb
White Horse Inn, Whitechapel 6Bc
White Horse Inn, Wood Street 5Ac
White Horse Lane, Mile End, Old Town 7Cb 8Ab 8Ac
White Horse Lane, White Horse Street 15Ca 16Aa
White Horse Passage, Great Swallow Street 10Aa
White Horse Street, Queen Street 16Bc 16Cc
White Horse Street, Ratcliff 16Aa
White Horse Yard, Chiswell Street, near Finsbury Mewse 5Bb
White Horse Yard, Chiswell Street, in Powels Alley 5Bb
White Horse Yard, Drury Lane 11Ba
White Horse Yard, Fans Alley 4Cb
White Horse Yard, Islington Road, St. John's Street 4Bb
White Horse Yard, Kent Street 21Ba
White Horse Yard, Pear Tree Street 4Ca
White Horse Yard, Piccadilly 10Bb
White Horse Yard, Pickax Street 4Cb
White Horse Yard, Radcliff Highway 14Bb 14Cb
White Horse Yard, Seething Lane 13Ca
White Lead Yard 16Cb
White Lion Court, Barbican 4Cb
White Lion Court, Barnaby Street 13Cc
White Lion Court, Birchin Lane 13Ba
White Lion Court, Blossom Street 6Ab
White Lion Court, Carpenters Yard, London Wall 5Bc
White Lion Court, Charterhouse Lane 4Cb 4Cc
White Lion Court, Cornhill 13Ba
White Lion Court, Fleet Street 12Aa
White Lion Court, Throckmorton Street 13Ba
White Lion Inn, near Lambeth Church 19Bb
White Lion Street, between Lemon Street and Rag Fair 14Ba
White Lion Wharf, Thames Street 12Ca
White Lion Yard, Barnaby Street 21Ca
White Lion Yard, Farmer Street, Upper Shadwell 15Bb
White Lion Yard, Narrow Street 16Bb
White Lion Yard, Norton Falgate 6Ab
White Lion Yard, Upper Shadwell 15Bb

White Rose Alley, Whitecross Street 5Ab
White Rose Court, Coleman Street 5Ac
White Street, Blackman Street 13Ac
White Street, Cutlers Street, Houndsditch 5Cc
White Street, Rotherhithe 15Ac 23Aa
White Swan Coachyard, Blackman Street 13Ac
White Swan Inn, Smithfield 4Bc
White Swan Inn, Whitechapel 14Ba
Whitehall 11Aa 11Ac
Whitehall Stairs 11Ac
Whitening Ground, near Maid Lane 12Cb
Whitening Ground, Morgans Lane 13Cb
White's Alley, Chancery Lane 4Ac
White's Alley, Coleman Street 5Bc
White's Alley, Holbourn 4Ac
White's Alley, Little Moorfields 5Bc
White's Alley, St. Catharine's Court, St. Catharine's 14Ab
White's Court, Vine Yard, St. Olaves Street 13Cc
White's Ground, Crucifix Lane 13Cc
White's Row, Bakers Row 6Cc
White's Row, Bell Lane 6Ac
White's Yard, Rosemary Lane and East Smithfield 14Bb 14Ba
White's Yard, Whitecross Street, Old Street 5Ab
Whittal's Rents, Long Lane 21Ba
Whittington College Alms Houses, College Hill 13Aa
Whores Nest, Harrow Corner 13Ab
Widegate Street, Bishopsgate Street 5Cc
Wiggan's Key, Thames Street 13Cb
Wigmore Row, Marybone Fields 1Cc
Wild Court, Great Wild Street 3Bc 11Ba
Wilderness, Dorset Street 12Ba
Wilderness Row, Chelsea 17Bc
Wild's Passage, Drury Lane 11Ba
Wild's Rents, Long Lane, Barnaby Street 21Ca
Willow Street, Bankside 12Cb 12Bb
Willow Tree Alley, Nightingale Lane 14Bb
Willow Tree Alley, Wapping Dock 15Ac
Willow Tree Court, Lower Shadwell 15Bb
Wilson's Alley, Fore Street, Lambeth 19Bb
Wiltshire Lane, East Smithfield 14Cb
Wimple Mewse, Wimple Street 1Cc
Wimple Street, Henrietta Street 1Cc
Winchester Court, Monkwell Street 5Ac
Winchester Street, Little Moorgate 5Bc
Winchester Street, St. Mary Overies 13Ab

Winchester Yard, Winchester Street 13Ab
Wincle's Court, Pall Mall 10Bb
Windmill Alley, St. Margaret's Hill 13Ac
Windmill Alley, Whitechapel 6Bc
Windmill, near Blackman Street, St. George's Fields 20Ca
Windmill Court, Coleman Street 5Ac
Windmill Court, Pye Corner 4Cc
Windmill Hill, Leather Lane 4Ab
Windmill Hill, Moorfields 5Bb
Windmill Hill Row, Upper Moorfields 5Bb
Windmill Inn, St. John Street 4Bb
Windmill Street, Haymarket 10Ca
Windmill Street, Tottenham Court Road 2Cb
Windsor Court, Drury Lane 11Ba
Windsor Court, Monkwell Street 5Ac
Wine Licence Office, Arundal Street 11Ca
Wine Office Court, Fleet Street 12Aa
Wine Street, Bedford Street, Liquor Pond Street 4Ab
Wingoose Alley, Thames Street 13Aa
Winkworth's Buildings, Austin Friers 5Bc
Winsley Street, Oxford Street 2Bc
Winston's Court, Silver Street, Wood Street 5Ac
Witchellors Yard, Thames Street 13Cb
Witherrush Court, White Cross Street 5Ab
Wood Street, Cheapside 5Ac 13Aa
Wood Street, Church Street, Spittlefields 6Ac 6Ab
Wood Street Counter 5Ac
Wood Street, Hare Street 6Cb
Wood Street, North Street, Westminster 19Aa
Wood Wharf, Fox Lane, Wapping 15Bb
Wood Yard, Brick Lane 6Bc
Wood Yard, Church Lane, Hounsditch 14Aa
Wood Yard, Farthing Alley, Maze Pond 13Bc
Wood Yard, Gravel Lane, Hounsditch 6Ac
Wood Yard, Moses and Aaron Alley 6Ac
Wood Yard, Princes Square, Ratcliff Highway 14Cb
Wood Yard, Redcross Street 13Ac
Woodroff Lane, Crutched Friers 14Aa
Wood's Close, near St. John's Street 4Ba 4Bb
Wood's Court, Norton Falgate 5Cb
Wood's Court, Oxford Street 2Bc
Wood's Mewse, Tyburn Lane 9Ba
Wood's Yard, Long Acre 11Aa
Woodstock Court, Charing Cross 11Ab
Woodstock Street, Oxford Street 9Ca